The Worl[illegible]rding to Enfield Senior

with an introduction by
Harry Enfield

illustrated by Geoff Waterhouse

Oldie Publications Ltd
London

This compilation first published by
Oldie Publications Ltd

The publishers would like to thank the respective copyright owners
for permission to include material in this volume

A CIP catalogue record for this book is available from
The British Library

Distribution by
World Leisure Marketing, 9 Downing Road,
West Meadows Industrial Estate, Derby DE21 6HA.
Tel: 01332 343332

ISBN 1-9011700-04-7

Cover illustration by John Kent
Design & production Richard Adams Associates
Text printed and bound by Woolnough Bookbinding Ltd
Covers printed by Amica Fine Art Print Ltd

Acknowledgements
Thanks to Richard Ingrams, James Pembroke, Marie Hemming,
Rory Campbell, Caroline Law, Richard Adams,
Anne Clark, Sam Adams and all at WLM.

Introduction by Harry Enfield

MY FATHER WAS born into the educated middle class. His father was a senior civil servant and his mother on the fringes of the Bloomsbury set. He grew up surrounded by the Good, the Great and the Slightly Odd.

My grandmother had a couple of books published by the Woolfs, even though Virginia Woolf detested her. She wrote in her diaries, upon hearing that the Stracheys were spending the afternoon with my grandparents: 'I would rather be dead in a field than have tea with the Enfields.'

In this atmosphere Dad was, I suspect, an ideal son – away a lot of the time. He was evacuated to Canada for the war, then went to Westminster and Oxford, where he read Classics. After Oxford he was about to take his Civil Service examinations when his mother died. He withdrew and took a job abroad, travelling the world and eventually meeting my mother in the Far East. They returned to England, my mother pregnant with my sister, in 1959.

Now with an embryonic family to support, he took a job with a pharmaceutical firm, where he remained for several years, my younger sister and I being born in the meantime. In 1967 he left his job, determined to become a lawyer, doing a correspondence course from home whilst we lived off his meagre savings. However, by September of that year he was forced to concede that the grinning little twits that interrupted him as he studied were a lot more expensive to rear than he had expected, and reluctantly he gave up his studies and took a post in the local education department where he remained until he retired in 1991.

Not only did my father give up his chosen career, but also most luxuries. We lived comparatively frugally, with every spare penny being spent on our education. It was his great hope that he would be able to give us the best possible start, so that we could have the type of fulfilment in our working lives that, by our premature existence, we had denied him. In this he was fully supported by my mother, whose childhood had been coloured by being constantly on the move as her father was posted round the world by the army. With a safe, stable homelife and the best education they could afford, their dream was that we would all become successful and financially secure professionals.

By 1976 it looked as if this dream would come to pass. My elder sister was soon to follow her father at Oxford, I had just turned fifteen, and had taken and passed my 'O' levels a year earlier than is normal, and my younger sisters were at the top of their classes in school.

But by 1991, my elder sister was a hippy living in a hut with a tribal husband and two babies in one of those West African countries you won't have heard of. My younger sister was a slightly bewildered semi-employed radio journalist. My youngest sister had recently embarked on a career making deceitful promotional videos for lost causes.

As for myself, the son and heir, I had used my expensive education to charm and cajole the successors of Lord Reith into giving me my own television programme, and now earn a tidy living from old-aged pensioners' licence fees by making people as idiotic as myself laugh, generally through the comic devices of swearing, shouting and pretending to break wind.

When in their mid twenties and thirties, none of my sisters had any financial security, and frequently nowhere to live either. Being comparatively well off myself, it would have been simple for me to help them out, but unfortunately, as is the rule with nouveau riche comedians, I am extremely mean and am happy to see my family reduced to grinding poverty as I watch my bank balance grow too large for the paper it is printed on.

At the start of 1992 my father noticed that along with my meanness, my vanity had also grown to new heights, causing me to shed two stone from the frame that until then I had been adorning with the flab of a thousand pointlessly expensive meals at the many vulgar restaurants which cater for London's upstarts.

He gingerly suggested that he would be prepared to spend many months ghost-writing a *Harry Enfield's Diet Book* which he was sure my 'excellent reputation' (I insist on flattery at all times nowadays) 'would make highly marketable', the proceeds going to my sisters to pay for their housing needs. All I had to do was agree to turn up for a day to have a few pictures of my beautiful self taken, and give his work to a publisher. Naturally my first thoughts were that I wasn't going to make a penny out of this arrangement, so I refused.

His next idea came from a discussion we had about Auberon Waugh's autobiography. He made the comment that many people who write their autobiographies spend a generous amount of time saying how awful their fathers were, and how they ruined their offspring's lives. He suggested that he would very much like to write about how awful his offspring were and how we

ruined his life. He wished to give the world an insight into the horrors of trying to bring up middle-class children in a civilised fashion, and seeing all one's efforts come to worse than nothing.

All four of us are a source of constant worry and embarrassment to our parents – 'What interesting children you have' is the veiled insult hurled at them daily by their friends. If there's one thing my father seeks to avoid more than his children, it is rows and confrontation. He has very rarely raised his voice to us.

The last time I remember him doing so was fifteen years ago when he came into my room to inform me, more in exasperation than anger, that my mother had been worried by the police coming round that day and recovering some property I happened to have stolen from a local shop. I met his enquiry by calling him and my mother every four-letter word I knew, over and over again until he stormed out of my room. A few minutes later he came back in and apologised for raising his voice to me. Quite right too.

Now he seems to think he'll be able to exercise his pent-up feelings of resentment through his pen. My natural reaction is to scoff at this idea. It seems to me that as none of his family has the slightest interest in anything he ever has to say, why should anyone else? Also, as age takes its toll, he is rapidly losing his grip on reality, and I doubt that there will be a shred of truth in anything he writes.

Nevertheless, to humour the old chap, I sent some of his stuff to Richard Ingrams who, purely to oblige me, said he'd find a space for it in *The Oldie*. I have arranged to intercept the greater part of his fee as my commission. So there's a little bit of extra drink money in it for me, and enough left over for him to buy me a passable Christmas present for a change.

13 November 1992

The Perils of Procreation

AH, THE CHILDREN! There are so many of them. Four, which seems to me to be a crowd. In fact, they are the reason why the house has five bedrooms. It only had three to start with, and we kept adding on bedrooms as we kept adding on children.

Sitting down six to every meal year after year is something which no one can understand unless they have been through it.

What is it about eating that leads to arguments? And why is it that table manners are so difficult? Why is it so hard to put a knife and fork down when not using them, and so much easier to wave them in the air? How long does it take to learn the trick of eating with a closed mouth?

If I were to look for a common bond between my children, it is that they all eat like savages.

Then there are their friends. When they were little, their friends were also little – little girls in neat pinafores who looked sweet, and little boys in shorts who said nothing and did what they were told. At least I think they were – it seems so at this distance in time.

Now their friends may have rings in their noses, and sprawl about the place and smoke and use foul language and sport Afro hairstyles, or else be skinheads.

When they are in the house I have to keep up a pretence of liking such people, which I am sure does not convince them. What am I supposed to have in common with a hippy female dangling the illegitimate offspring of an out-of-work Rastafarian? Nothing, of course, so why is she doing it on the sofa in our drawing-room?

Occasionally, there is one that is reasonably clean and tolerably presentable, but I cannot say anything nice about him or her because I have not said it about the arrogant Oxford-educated puppy with holes in the knees of his jeans that I felt like kicking out of the front door. If I am nice about one but silent about the other, they want to know why I did not like the other, and if I tell them, they tell me I am wrong.

Paternal Protocol

My son tells me that on television you get sons saying they love their fathers, and what do I think of that?

Well, I think it could only happen in America. I have seen the sort of thing he means, and it goes something like this:

Son: I love you, Dad.

Father: And I love you, Son.

This does not seem to me to be true to life. Much more natural would be:

Son: I love you, Dad.

Father: How very embarrassing!

Even this is only half true. Absolute truth would require:

Son: You're a bore, Dad.

Father: And you're a liability, Son.

Yet this too has only a superficial veracity. What you actually get is:

Son: How are you, Dad?

Father: I'm fine, Son.

It does not do to crack the veneer of civilisation which must overlay family life if it is to remain tolerable.

A Plague of Prurience

What the arts need just now is a good dose of censorship. I said this to my sister-in-law, who is a woman of a liberal turn of mind, and not quite knowing how to deal with this illiberal idea, she said: 'Who would do the censoring?'

This seems a very easy question to answer. Any reasonably sensible person could do it, and if no one else wants to, I will, and I will do it for stage, cinema, television, books and anything you like.

First of all I would censor out all cruelty. There are some human tastes which are so beastly that they ought to be starved, and the taste for cruelty is one of them. I never go to films about the navy in the days of sail because I know they will flog someone; or about the Middle Ages because they will torture someone. Under my regime that sort of thing would stop.

After that I would cut out all nudity, obscenity, blasphemy, indecency, and any jokes that failed to make me laugh. The result would be that I would be hailed as the saviour of the British film industry, as all films made in this country would be made to the standard of *Chariots of Fire*, and be immensely popular both here and abroad.

Pilfered Plots

Plagiarism is a funny thing.

A man called David Lodge, whom the *Daily Telegraph* sometimes calls Prof

Lodge, wrote a book called *Nice Work*, having pinched the plot from Mrs Gaskell. A woman called Pauline Harris, who the *Telegraph* says is sometimes called Rachel Ford, wrote a book called *The Iron Master*, with a plot, it seems, much like that of *Nice Work*.

'You have pinched my plot!' says Prof Lodge.

'Not a bit,' says Mrs Harris. I pinched it from Mrs Gaskell, where you pinched yours.'

'Oh, that's all right then,' says Prof Lodge.

So it seems that pinching plots from Mrs Gaskell is not plagiarism, but pinching plots that have been pinched from Mrs Gaskell is. As I say, plagiarism is a funny thing.

27 November 1992

Christmas is the Worst

'What are you doing for Christmas?'
'Well, the children will be coming home'.
'That will be nice.'

NO, IT WILL not be nice, it will be terrible. There will be nowhere to go because every room will be full of young people either watching rubbish on television, or talking rubbish and laughing a lot. This makes it impossible for me to read, and there is nothing going on which tempts me to join in.

If I say 'I am going for a walk', there is a risk of somebody saying they will come too. If they say they are going for a walk, I say I will stay and keep the fire going, but there is a risk of someone staying to keep me company. If I go up to my bedroom or sneak out for a walk on my own, they start to worry in case I have gone mad. They have reason to worry, of course, not because I have gone mad but because they have driven me mad, just as there is all the difference between taking to drink and being driven to drink.

It says in the *Dictionary of National Biography* that the great nineteenth-century classical scholar Richard Porson in his later years 'gave way to

intemperance'. Nowadays he would have a drink problem, but they did things properly in those days. While I do not think I am ever likely to have a drink problem, at Christmas I am strongly tempted to give way to intemperance.

The present-giving is a nightmare. The rule is that not a single present may be opened until some event has taken place. The nature of the event has varied with time. Originally it was that everyone had been to church, but, when this became unenforceable, it was that everyone who was going to church had been to church. Finally, when the children were of an age to refuse to go to church, en bloc, as an act of solidarity against their mother, it was when the turkey was in the oven.

The number of presents to be exchanged has increased over the years in arithmetical or possibly geometrical progression with the addition of each child, because everybody has to give everybody a present. To calculate the minimum number of presents changing hands, let X be the number in the family and P the number of presents. The formula is: P=X (X-1).

With a family of six, everyone gives a present to everyone but themselves, so each will give five presents, bringing the total to 6 x 5 = 30. To this has to be added the contributions of grandparents and the aunt who stays for Christmas and thereby increases the value of X. The value of grandparents is a little difficult to assess, but allowing 1 for grandparents and 1 for the resident aunt, for a family of six the total value of X is 8, which means that at least 56 presents are given and received. This is further increased by casual donations from godmothers, non-resident aunts, best friends and others.

In the interval between the turkey going into the oven and the turkey coming out again, parcel after parcel is ripped from its expensive wrapping, glanced at, a smile is forced, thanks simulated, and on to the next one, till the room is knee-deep in paper and Sellotape, and everyone has a small pile of clothes they can change if they want to, books they can change if they want to, and a mixture of sweets, knick-knacks, kitchen utensils, bric-à-brac, toys, food, drink, plants, and, if they are lucky, cash. My son usually gives me a packet of pipe-cleaners although I do not smoke, and says it is just a token and that the real present will follow, which it never does.

I am sure that this is not how Christmas was meant to be. Christmas has come to be celebrated by louts kicking empty beer-cans round the centre of the cathedral city where I used to work, by drunkenness on a grand scale, by an orgy of expenditure, by supposedly comic and undeniably smutty programmes on television, and by family occasions which, once they are over, everyone admits they did not enjoy a bit.

11 December 1992

My Disgustingly Coarse Son

THEY SAY THAT old men always think that things were better when they were young. This does not mean that the old men are wrong, it just means that nobody takes any notice of them. One of the things that I can see getting worse is the way people either make up new words when there are perfectly good words already, or use words to mean things they cannot mean, just because they are too mealy-mouthed to use the right words.

The other night, after the news, the TV announcer warned me that the next programme contained 'explicit language'. I knew what he meant so I turned it off, but most language is explicit. If I say, 'I would like to buy this packet of frozen peas,' that is as explicit as anything, but the shop assistant does not shriek and run away. What the TV people meant was that the language was obscene or blasphemous, or most probably obscene and blasphemous, which has nothing to do with being explicit.

Then I read in the paper that *The Archers* has become a 'steamy raunchy soap'. There is no such word as 'raunchy', but they made it up as a namby-pamby synonym for 'lewd'. The steamy soap bit sounds vaguely reminiscent of a launderette, whereas by a steamy raunchy soap they mean a lewd and vulgar serial, and they ought to say so.

It is of course a sign of the total failure of all my efforts that my son's performances could frequently be introduced with the words, 'The next programme contains scenes of gross indecency and the language is disgustingly coarse and frequently blasphemous'. The trouble is, now that I suggest it, he will probably do it, and people will think it is a joke and a laugh.

25 December 1992

Eminent Enfields

OUR FIRST CHILD was a daughter. I said to my father that I thought he might have preferred a grandson to carry on the family name. 'Why?' he said, 'Little girls are much nicer than boys.' I took this to mean that he thought my sister was much nicer than me, but later on we had a son, and I began to see what he meant.

As a boy, I used to go to the public library in Hampstead and borrow the *Mother West Wind* stories. I have yet to meet anyone else who has read them. They were always the same. An animal would be created and turned out into the world for a year, at the end of which time it was allowed to ask for one gift from Mother West Wind.

The ones I remember were the gopher, which asked for pockets in its cheeks to store the earth when it was tunnelling, and the hare, which asked to go white in winter so that it could hide in the snow. As there are no gophers in England and as English hares stay brown in winter, I now think the stories must have been American, but nobody told me this so I believed that the earth under my feet was being hollowed out by gophers, and at the first fall of snow all the hares went white.

Anyway, the Mother West Wind idea has always seemed to me to be excellent, and ever since I read the stories I have been wondering what I should have asked for if I had the chance. To sing like Pavarotti? To ride like Johnny Francome? To have a memory like Lord Macaulay? I tried the idea on an American friend who said that she would ask for a Background, which seemed to me a very surprising answer and one which might have puzzled Mother West Wind.

Well, the Enfields are not troubled by a shortage of background. The family goes back to the year 1741 when Dr William Enfield LLD was born. It says in the introduction to his sermons that 'his parents were in a humble condition of life which they rendered respectable by their virtues.'

Dr Enfield, who was a Unitarian clergyman, had his portrait painted twice, and this was a cause of great aggravation nearly two centuries later between my father and his elder brother, whom he cordially disliked.

By my grandfather's will my uncle was left a pair of portraits of Dr and Mrs Enfield, and my father a single portrait of Dr Enfield. My uncle said he had not room for two, and asked my father to swap his one for my uncle's pair, which sounded like a bargain to my father, so he agreed. Later on, he got the idea that the single portrait he had parted with was by Raeburn, whereas the pair were by someone unknown, so he was full of resentment at the way his brother had cheated him.

However, he had his two portraits cleaned by a Mr Drown of Bond Street, who declared that they were by Gainsborough, and then my father was full of glee at the way my uncle had cheated himself. There was not a grain of truth in either of these theories.

Later on my uncle gave his Raeburn to me, and it has a label on the back saying, 'Dr Enfield, by Williamson'. The Gainsboroughs were viewed by a man from the National Gallery who declared that they had nothing whatsoever to do with Gainsborough.

The Enfields have achieved greatness, or more recently notoriety, in alternate generations. Both Dr William Enfield and his grandson Edward appear in the *Dictionary of National Biography*; my father in *Who's Who*; and my son in the *TV Times*. I am of the generation that slumbers.

8 January 1993

On the Box

IT WAS PERHAPS a good idea to put a man from television in charge of prisons, but it would have been a better one to put a man from the prison service in charge of television. If half the BBC drama department were banged up three to a cell with alternative comedians and anyone who had anything to do with *Prime Suspect* or *Pallas*, they would discover at slopping out time what it was like for the rest of us to be exposed to their nastiness.

The man I feel really sorry for is A N Wilson. He is the television critic of the *Sunday Telegraph*, and if ever a man was unhappy in his work he is, as he hates everything except the repeats of *Dad's Army*. He got carried away at Christmas when he vented his spleen on the religious broadcasts, to which he says only a tiny proportion of audiences are sympathetic. This is easy to check, and it did not cost me much trouble to find out that six million people watched *Harry Enfield's Festive TV Programme*, but nine million watched Christmas *Morning Worship*, which speaks well for the good sense of the British people and proves that you cannot believe what you read, even in the *Sunday Telegraph*.

Otherwise I am more or less with A N Wilson. I watched Clive Anderson's chat show for no better reason than that my son was on it. When I say that it improved when he came on, it will be clear that it was not my kind of thing.

After this I noticed that the show jumping had got put back to 11pm. Surely the pornographers cannot have got hold of that, I thought, so I put it on to see. I am happy to report that it is perfectly decent, but it is different from when I last saw it. There used to be a man with adenoids who told you what you had just seen for yourself.

If a horse hit a jump and it fell down, he said 'Oh, it's gone!', and if it didn't fall he said, 'Got away with it!' Nowadays they let you see without telling you what you have seen, but they chatter all the time. 'She's took a lot of flak;' 'he unfolded a bit quick;' 'he jumped well at Bordeaux, but that's in France and this is England.' There was a certain amount of mind-reading ('Tina's got tomorrow in mind') which used to be done for the horses as well. In the old days, the horses had sporting names, something like 'Harvey's Reasonably Priced Amontillado Sherry', perhaps known as 'Monty' for short, and Adenoids would declare: 'Monty shakes his head to say "That was a tricky one" '. I wondered how he knew. If I had been Monty, it might have meant 'If I could get the beggar off, I'd roll on him.'

22 January 1993

The Thrill of the Chase

WHAT MY WIFE, who is Irish, really dislikes about her countrymen is their Irishness, which is a quality one can only describe by example. We once asked a man called Gorman to dinner and he arrived an hour and a half late, keeping the other guests and ourselves waiting. His method of apologising was to exclaim in a boisterous manner as he came through the door, 'If this was a quiz, could you guess which was the Irishman in the party?' Those who suffer from Irishness either think that, being Irish, they cannot be expected to be punctual or, more likely, unpunctuality is part of their Irish charm.

My wife is perfectly punctual, but she cannot escape certain Irish characteristics, such as wild exaggerated pessimism. If it is possible to look on the black side, that is the side to look on. When thirsty she says, 'I'd give anything for a glass of water.' In fact, as far as she is concerned, it is free, as I have paid the water rates, but this has no effect. Similarly things in our house are never clean or dirty, they are always filthy or spotless, and the house itself is never warm or cold, it is boiling or freezing.

The reason my wife is Irish is that her parents were. They were Catholics from Cork, with the unlikely names of Jenkins and Bennett. (Bennett was my mother-in-law's maiden name – I do not mean to imply that my wife is illegitimate).

My mother-in-law was very keen on clothes and fashion but she did not have much money, largely owing to my father-in-law's agreeable Irish fecklessness. She dealt with this by hunting for bargains at sales, an activity which she raised to the level of an Olympic sport. By 'sales' I mean things like Harrods' sale, which in those days was a real sale and not the poor thing it is now. Before the Egyptians got hold of it they never bought anything in, they just reduced the prices of the stock in hand.

If things did not sell at the reduced prices they reduced them again, and if they still did not sell, they reduced them yet again. On the last day of the sale, in order to shift the stuff that was left they brought the prices down dramatically, and that was my mother-in-law's big moment.

All year round she would prowl through Harrods like a hungry tigress, marking down the likely items which seemed to be sticking in the shop and were therefore candidates for the sale. She called this process 'watching'.

On the first day of the sale she would be there, doing a bit more watching, but never buying. As the sale progressed and prices came down but goods disappeared, she would become more and more excited and nervous, wondering whether to move in on a coveted item or to risk waiting for a further reduction.

It was not exactly a blood sport, though knowing the speed with which she moved through the crowds armed with an umbrella I expect there were some casualties. It had, however, a certain similarity to fox hunting, in which it is not uncommon for the huntsman to throw the reins of his horse to someone else to hold, while he plunges among the hounds to perform the last rites on the fox. In the same way my mother-in-law would fling my wife, then a babe in arms, to a shop assistant with instructions to hold her while she moved in for the kill, or as she herself put it, while she 'pounced'.

I have to say that this tireless pursuit of bargains meant she was always strikingly and elegantly attired. She had a certain vanity about her appearance, and always considered that any picture of herself was spoilt if my wife, as a child, got into it. She used then to cut her out with scissors and throw her away, and my wife has a number of photographs of her mother which have holes in them for this reason.

5 February 1993

Army Logic

I DID MY National Service in Germany, in a supposedly Irish regiment, namely the Eighth King's Royal Irish Hussars. It is now defunct, having been merged and re-merged with other regiments.

The number of Irishmen in the army varies from time to time. In parts of the nineteenth century conditions were so bad that only Irishmen would enlist, and the Welsh Fusiliers were Irish to a man (and perhaps to a goat as well, as they have a regimental goat). As Englishmen had to do National Service while Irishmen did not, there were only a few Irishmen in the Eighth Hussars. They kept up the regimental Irishness by wearing hats embroidered with shamrocks and calling their squadrons 'R', 'B' and 'C'. 'R' squadron was spelt 'A' squadron but pronounced 'R' as Irishmen are supposed to be unable to say 'A' and always say 'R', or 'Ah', as you prefer . . .

They also had a lot of horses, housed in a magnificent stable block built for the German Panzer regiment, whose barracks had been taken over. Keeping horses is an Irish trait all right, but in this case it was more to do with being a cavalry regiment, and they certainly did not have more horses than their predecessors, the Royal Scots Greys. The Eighth Hussars, when posted to Germany to relieve the Greys, took over from them the barracks, the tanks and the horses. The tanks were found to be in very bad condition, and it was explained that 'the Greys don't like starting the tanks, as it frightens the horses'.

The horses were kept purely for pleasure and not for any military or ceremonial purposes. They were looked after by a mixture of German grooms who were on the payroll as clerks and storemen, and Eighth Hussars troopers.

There are those who argue for the return of National Service on account of the moral uplift it conveyed which, for those who spent two years of service to Queen and country in mucking out the horses ridden by the officers of the Eighth Hussars, may not have been very great.

The colonel was not an Irishman, but an Englishman with an estate in Wales, whom I remember as being short of breath and talking like a character called Jogglebury Crowdey in the novels of Surtees. I was present when he disciplined a trooper called Fulleylove for punching Sergeant Hooley on the nose at an Other Ranks' Dance. Fulleylove's problem was that he wanted to marry a German girl, and the colonel wouldn't let him, on the grounds that no decent German girl would go out with a British soldier, and he wasn't having any of his men marrying tarts. In punching Sergeant Hooley, Fulleylove was actually trying to punch his way out of the army with a dishonourable discharge. Sergeant Hooley, who was Irish, gave his evidence:

'Sorr,' he said, 'on the day and date stated, sorr, I observed the accused creating a disturbance, sorr. I approached him and remonstrated with him, sorr. Five minutes later I observed the same occurrence occurring again, and I approached the accused and he struck me. Sorr!'

'Well Fulleylove,' said the colonel, 'what have you got to say?'

'Nothing to say, sir,' said Fulleylove gloomily.

'Well, Fulleylove,' said the colonel. 'You're a swine,' (wheeze). 'Sergeant Hooley and I were your guests,' (gasp) 'and we don't go to parties,' (puff) 'to be hit by our hosts.' (wheeze) 'Twenty-eight days. March out!'

I could not see any flaw in the colonel's logic, as hosts certainly should not hit their guests, but I think Fulleylove might have understood better if the colonel had called it 'striking a superior officer'. Still, army logic was generally interesting. I was in the adjutant's office when they made an inventory of the furniture. There was a little coffee table which to me was just a little coffee table, but it went into the inventory as 'Tables, nest of three, two deficient.'

19 February 1993

Name Dropping

WHEN YOU HAVE children you have to give them names, which is a difficult matter and should be done with care. It seems to me now that we just blundered into it without proper consideration and things might have turned out differently if we had studied the subject more closely. I have always believed that Abraham Lincoln achieved greatness because he had such an excellent name, part of which is due to the rhythm, a dactyl and a spondee, (Ābrăhăm Līncōln, like that). Had I realised the importance of this I would have called our son Algernon, as Algernon Enfield has just the right cadence. So does Benjamin Enfield, and Benjamin is a good name, as Benjamin was the last born. This is a nice thought, but it would not have done for us as Ben Enfield sounds perilously like an alternative comedian and this would just have brought us round full circle, more or less.

When trying out a name for size, it is as well to experiment with a few prefixes and suffixes. Sir Algernon Enfield, QC, sounds well, as does Sir Algernon and Lady Enfield. I can imagine General Algernon Enfield, MC, or Algernon Enfield, OM. Any one of these would have been more what we had in mind than what we have actually got. Too late I realised that you can give a child a leg up in the world at no extra cost to yourself by making the second name St John or de Courcy, or both if you are confident of having only one offspring. They never need use these names but it makes a difference to their initials. J St J Brown is altogether superior to J Brown – likewise P de C Smith to P Smith, and A St J de C Jones to either of them.

If I had studied the family tree more closely I would have got some better ideas for our children, because we are connected with the Dowson family, who had some good notions about names. There was one called Septimus Dowson (note the rhythm). The thought of seven children makes me shudder, but having a system does save thought and time. Had we adopted the Latin numerical approach and simply called our children Prima, Secundus, Tertia and Quarta it would have been far easier to remember who they all are and where they fit into the hierarchy.

But the name I really liked in the family tree was Withers Dowson. I thought the system of naming one's children after the points of a horse was both original and interesting, and I searched the family tree for Fetlock Dowson or Forelock Dowson, but in vain. Having hit on the idea, for some reason they gave it up. What, I wonder, would have been the effect of calling my son Foreleg Enfield? Quite a theatrical name perhaps, and certainly good for steady parts in pantomine. As it is we gave our children quite ordinary names and cast them adrift upon the world like little evacuees labelled Sue and Harry, Lizzie and Lucy.

No Son of Mine?

I wonder whether my son could possibly be a changeling, having muddled up his labels in hospital. That is just the sort of thing he would do, and it would explain a lot. Out there, perhaps, is the son we always wanted, a clean-living, well-spoken, pin-striped solicitor, regularly driven to the station in the Volvo by his pretty wife, before she take Piers and Antonia to school. If anyone has such a young man, born in Horsham towards the end of May 1961, could they please get in touch. Admittedly the prospect of changing him for a chain-smoking, sloppily-dressed comic who needs a haircut is not attractive, but the rewards could be substantial. I am told the tabloids of the lower sort would gladly pay £100,000 for the exclusive right to the 'I swapped my son for Harry Enfield' story. We would not want a share, as to unite my wife with the son of her dreams would be reward enough.

5 March 1993

Played Out

I TOOK MY wife to the theatre a few weeks ago, which is always a dangerous thing for me to do. Theatre managements would be well advised to refuse to let us in, or at least to make us carry a warning. The thing is, I do not really like actors. There is too much of the you-sit-down-there-and-be-quiet-while-I-prance-about-up-here for my liking, and it takes a good play to get my mind off the performers.

The result is that my wife and I together can cast a gloom over an entire evening, not just for us but for everybody. Sure-fire things like *West Side Story* or *Oh What A Lovely War* fall as flat as pancakes when we are there, and Sir Alec Guinness would gladly swap us for several rows of Japanese, anytime.

This time it was *Trelawney of the Wells* and, contrary to custom, it was superb. It had Sarah Brightman and little Miss Bonham-Carter and it should have had Michael Hordern but he was ill, which did not matter at all as a man called Kauffman took his place and was excellent. Almost the best part was after the end, which is the bit I usually hate the most. Instead of coming on in dribs and drabs to be clapped, and going off and coming back till the last dregs of applause have been drained from the audience, the whole lot arrived in a bunch, Sarah Brightman gave us a lovely smile, then they all went away and we could all go home.

Play-going reminiscences are not much in my line, but the best thing I ever saw was Lorraine Chase in *Pygmalion*. I knew about Lorraine Chase because she used to appear on a panel game called *Blankety Blank*, which I always watched when she was on because she was so beautiful and quick-witted. When I heard she was to be in *Pygmalion* I toiled all the way up to London to see it, which is a most unusual way for me to behave. The reason was that while Bernard Shaw probably thought he wrote the part for Mrs Patrick Campbell or someone like that, I could see at once that he really wrote it for Lorraine Chase. Other actresses have ladylike voices and put on what they believe to be cockney accents for the part but Miss Chase has quite the most excruciating natural voice you ever heard and was going to have to do it the other way round, like Eliza Doolittle.

Well I hope Bernard Shaw was able to watch it from the grave, because it was magnificent. The first time Eliza was to use her new voice they managed to give Miss Chase about a minute and a half of walking-on time. She stalked slowly across the stage with her wonderful mannequin walk, while we sat on the edge of our seats not daring to breathe, until she held out her hand and said, 'How do you do?' – when the whole theatre exploded into cheering and applause.

But from the best of times to the worst of times. These started when my wife took our then twelve-year-old daughter to a 'new thriller' in Guildford.

'What was it like?' I asked when they got back.

'Terrible. It was full of filthy foul language, and half way through the second act some man took off all his clothes and jumped around with nothing on.'

'Oh dear,' said I, 'but never mind. I have found that Alistair Sim is on in Brighton, and Alistair Sim in Brighton must be safe enough for Terence Rattigan's aunt or anyone else, even us.'

So off we went to Brighton and the play was full of filthy foul language and half way through the second act some man took off all his clothes and started jumping about with nothing on.

But I did not wish to be beaten, so when I found that the Vienna Boys Choir was to sing in Chichester I bought tickets for that, having first made quite sure at the box office that all the boys kept all their clothes on all the time.

19 March 1993

Subs' Standards

I FIND I have become a columnist, but I was not sure how to pronounce it. Do you sound the 'n'? It must be there for some purpose, and while you cannot sound it if all you are saying is 'column', you do if you say 'columnar'. I decided to give the 'n' something to do, and say columNist, like that.

No sooner had I settled that to my satisfaction than Valerie Grove (Wireless) told me to parade for interview for the *Times*, and to bring my son. We went to a dingy rendezvous in the seediest part of Soho, where she asked me the following shrewd and penetrating question: 'Do you get lonely when you are alone?' 'Never,' I replied. '*Numquam minus solus quam cum solus.*'

Result – chaos. It means, of course, 'Never less alone than when alone', and I wish I could add 'as every schoolboy knows', but they are too busy with their hands-on computer literacy lessons to learn to construe a simple piece of Latin.

It had a terrible effect upon the *Times*. That paper, I discovered, is staffed by half-educated people called Subs, one of whom said he thought that I had got it wrong. They have a man called Philip Howard who is hired to settle points of classical learning (which is clearly better than referring them to the proprietor), but he had gone absent. It threw them into a panic. I told them it was from Cicero and in the end they rather grudgingly accepted Cicero as a good enough authority, though they would have been happier with Philip Howard.

Shortly afterwards the phone rang again. It was the *Evening Standard* wanting me to go to London to see and interview a one-man stand-up transvestite comic. They said he was entirely wholesome and quite unlike my son, so I agreed. Even so, it did not seem to be my scene.

'We will send a limousine to drive you to London – it will wait, and drive you back to Sussex,' said the *Standard*. Extraordinary behaviour! I asked if it would do if I stayed the night. 'A great idea!' they cried, 'we will book you into the Waldorf.'

So I stayed at the Waldorf, where they give you a complimentary *Daily Telegraph* in a sealed plastic bag, which makes it very difficult to get at. They also give you complimentary soap and lend you a complimentary towel and present you with a pretty handsome complimentary bill.

I went to see the comedian. He was privately educated, and one sentence in the printed programme starts 'Me and my big brother went off to another boarding school…', which shows you that the fees did not cover elementary grammar. I sat, a small island of gloom in an ocean of juvenile hilarity, until the show was over and I could go and talk to him. I was right. It was not my scene.

I was woken next day by the Waldorf Dalek. It rings you up and says 'Have a good day' instead of 'Exterminate'. Then I filed my copy. At least I think that is what I did with it. I read it down the phone to a man called Dave, who typed it out. We were Dave and Edward from the start. At the end of each phrase Dave would say 'Yes' or 'Right', to show that he had got it down, so it went something like this:

Edward: My son's live shows were awful…

Dave: Yes.

Edward: …because he was so coarse…

Dave: Yes.

Edward: …so I never went to see them.

Dave: Right.

It was as if everything I said met with absolute approval from first to last.

Later I rang them up, and they said they were going to run it on Monday, as if they had entered it in a horse race. Then they scratched it for Monday and said they would run it on Tuesday. It did not run on Tuesday and I did not hear any more, so I thought perhaps they thought it was lame and had withdrawn it altogether. Then they ran it a week later. It is all material for my great unwritten novel *On The Spike*, which will take the lid off the world of journalism.

2 April 1993

Child's Play

IT IS YEARS since I have been to a children's party, or to a school play, but now that my eldest granddaughter is five years old I begin to fear that there might be dangers in that direction. I have tried my hand at many things which have not turned out well, but my efforts at running children's parties ranked among my more conspicuous failures. Either we devised a series of 20 games, which they got through at the rate of one a minute and were then hanging about shouting 'What are we going to do now?' – or we got a conjurer and they saw through every trick and explained it in a chorus to my wife and me, who were the only ones who could not see how it was done. Some fell upon the tea like ravening wolves, and others would not eat so much as a biscuit. Either way it did not take long, and we were always left with an hour to go and no idea what to do.

Quite clearly nursery school teachers have a harder job, and should be paid more than anyone else, as they solve this problem for five days a week and 38 weeks a year. We thankfully sent our children to nursery school at the first opportunity for as long as possible, and after that they went to a school distinguished by the fact that it put on the worst school play in the kingdom, every year.

We all delude ourselves, but I have never known such extraordinary self-deception as that by which the headmistress convinced herself that the parents enjoyed watching the thing, when actually we all hated it. So firmly was she under the misconception that it was an enjoyable spectacle that a special performance was mounted for the suffering residents of the local Old People's Home who, according to the headmistress, regarded it as the high spot of their year, whereas it was certainly the low spot of ours, and therefore probably of theirs.

Few professional actors can act, and almost no amateurs, so amateur theatricals are things to avoid, above all if done by children. The headmistress's idea was to give every child in the school a part, so there was a cast of about 140 without, at that age, a scrap of talent between them.

Originally the mothers had to make the costumes. They were told that their child was to be Tweedledum or the Angel Gabriel or a rabbit or a fairy, and they were to dress them accordingly. The costumes were left on the mothers' hands after the play and just thrown away, with new ones made every year. Eventually the mothers rebelled and one of them was made to be wardrobe mistress and ordered to take that year's costumes into store and issue them out again next year. This had the effect that, whatever the play, whether a Nativity play, *Hansel and Gretel* or *Alice in Wonderland*, the same old bluebirds, elves, squirrels and fairies came hopping across the stage in just the same way as they had done last year and would do next year.

Three episodes from these plays stick in my mind. The first is comprised in two lines from *Hiawatha* who, according to this play, was by parentage a hybrid, out of an Indian squaw by the West Wind. The manner in which Hiawatha was conceived was explained in the lines:

And the West Wind came and caught her
Bending down among the lilies

– which I thought was much too explicit for the mouths of babes and sucklings. The second was when the dancing mistress was mistakenly given a free hand, and put a lot of little girls into grass skirts and made them do a hula dance, which may have appealed to the paedophiles in the audience but shocked the rest of us. Far the most vivid moment however was when the Snow Queen, at the height of the action, opened her mouth and was sick, leaving my son, a fat and red-faced blue tit, dancing round the resultant mess with evident distaste.

A lot of grandparents have to be dragooned into school play audiences in order to make up numbers. I really feel I have done my time, and owe no further debt to society, but if I must, I must. I just hope they don't make Katie the Snow Queen.

Just Put Your Lips Together...

My neighbour's granddaughter can whistle. This may not seem to be anything special until I say that she is only eleven months old, and has been doing it for several weeks. I have not got too wide an acquaintance among babies, but I have known a few in my time, and never met a whistling one before. I thought at first that she must whistle like a parrot, which, of course, cannot purse up its beak, so it has to whistle with its vocal cords. Not Olivia – she whistles properly, like an errand boy.

Her favourite place for whistling is in church. She is a Catholic, and while

Father Gordon intones at the front, Olivia lies in a pew at the back, and whistles. She particularly liked the Feast of the Epiphany as she thought that all the extra people must have come to hear the famous whistling baby, and so she ran through her repertoire, from whistling *piano e dolce* to whistling *forte con brio*. The fans loved it.

I used to think that only boys could whistle. Indeed, had I been looking for a whistler I might have interviewed a girl or two, but only to avoid being taken to an industrial tribunal, not because I thought they stood a chance. I would have been quite wrong. Give her another year and I reckon Olivia will be able to call you a cab as well as any doorman in Britain. She must be the youngest Women's Libber in the kingdom.

16 April 1993

I Once Met...

FIELD MARSHAL SIR William Slim, KCB, GCMG, DSO, MC as he then was, once addressed a remark to me and 1,499 other people which I have remembered for over 40 years.

It was at Catterick camp, where I went in 1952 to start my national service. They gave us all sub-lethal doses of typhoid, cholera and lockjaw, and ordered us to sit on our beds and polish our boots and brasses, and not to stop till they told us. When we began to regain our health they started us on foot drill, and from then on we divided our time between foot drill and polishing. We polished and wore our second-best boots, and we polished our best boots but never wore them. For six weeks nobody spoke a civil word to us except some ladies from the blood transfusion service who came to extract a pint from each of us.

Then they told us that the CIGS was coming to see us. They did not tell us what a CIGS was, or whether it was a group or a person, but the news sent a shiver of excitement through the whole camp of, I guess, about 1,500 men, and six NAAFI girls. It also caused them to step up the foot drill and the polishing.

We learned that when the CIGS comes to see you the thing to do is march around in circles. A box was put on the barrack square on which the CIGS would stand, and for hour upon hour we practised marching in circles in front of it. Then we went back and polished some more.

When the day came we got up early so as not to be late, and actually put our best boots on our feet instead of on top of our lockers. It was the first of about six occasions in two years on which those boots were worn. We fell in at seven o'clock and marched to the barrack square, which took about 10 minutes. Then we waited. Punctually at 11 o'clock a helicopter arrived and a man got out, who I later learned was Bill Slim. He got on the box and, as arranged, we marched around in circles. Then he made a speech.

The opening words of this speech comprised the memorable statement of which I have spoken. 'The infantry,' he said, 'is the backbone of the army.' This theme he went on to develop, and it may not seem at all remarkable until I explain that Catterick camp was entirely given over to the Royal Armoured Corps and the Royal Corps of Signals, and of the 1,500 of us on parade there was not a single infantryman present.

But we did not hiss or boo this man who had just told us we were of no account. We did not even throw down our caps and waistbelts and declare 'We'll soldier no more, you may do what you please,' as in the example given in the manual of military law. On the contrary, on the command 'Remove headdress' we removed our headdress, and on the command 'Hip, hip' we raised the headdress to the full extent of the right arm, shouted 'Hooray!', counted a pause of – two – three, and returned the headdress to the region of the left breast. We did this three times. Then the CIGS remounted his helicopter and rode away, and we marched back to barracks to repair the damage to our best boots.

30 April 1993

Horse Power

I HAVE GREAT sympathy for the poor man who failed to wave the flag at the Grand National. I know exactly how he felt as I once did something similar myself.

It was to do with the Pony Club, which is an institution from which I suffered a good deal because of my daughters, who all had ponies and went in for the Pony Club in one way or another. The Pony Club fell to me rather than my wife because I had had dealings with horses in the past, but normally ponies are women's work, like cooking.

There are a great many women who like horses as long as they do not have to get on their backs. To them horses and ponies are large animated dolls to be dressed, fed, put to bed, got out of bed, taken around the place and talked about interminably. They do not like getting on their backs because they might fall off, and while all horsey women will deny this the Argu-mentum Rice Davies applies.

Because they do not want to ride themselves they make their daughters do it. Their sons, generally speaking, refuse. The daughters, being potential women, behave in a similar sort of way to their mothers, but are braver about the riding. They are not, however, generally as brave on their own account as their mothers are on their behalf. The sort of thing one hears quite often is some mother hissing between clenched teeth at her blubbering, terrified offspring: 'You will get on and you will BLOODY WELL JUMP!'

Horsey women can be like that – fiercely ambitious and often foul mouthed, which is but background to the episode I have compared to the Grand National, intended to convey that a congregation of Pony Club mothers is every bit as formidable as a horde of angry punters at Aintree.

My personal disaster happened at a thing called a One Day Event, at which I was the chief scorer, out of three. It was a very grand affair, and ponies came from far and wide. I tried to compute the cash value of the ponies, horse boxes, Range Rovers, BMWs, trailers, saddlery and general dressing-up gear, and passed the £1 million mark with ease. Every animal had to go in for three separate competitions for each of which it could get bad marks, and we had to add up the bad marks. Whoever got the fewest would win, and whichever team got the fewest would go to a place called Stoneleigh, which is a sort of horsey Valhalla to which all Pony Club women wish their daughter to go.

All day long the three of us sat in a caravan with children thrusting bits of paper at us with numbers on them, and these we copied down and added up, until at last through sheer tedium we put down the number written on a child's back, which was 120, instead of its bad marks, which were nil. Everything was totalled, results announced, cups presented, rosettes distributed, applause raised for those going to Valhalla, and everyone was about to go home when a tearful creature arrived at the caravan to ask why she had been given a cricket score when she had not done a thing wrong. Her team, instead of being nowhere, had actually won. Everything had to be undone, the cups taken away, the rosettes seized back, those that thought they were going to Valhalla told they were not going anywhere, and I had more or less to be smuggled out with a coat over my head, like a child molester.

On the strength of this experience I am proposing to start a club called the Fiasco Society. I am inviting as founder members whoever the Jockey Club decides were responsible at Aintree, and the Cambridge cox who rammed a barge on Boat Race day. We will dine annually at the Savoy, after inducting as a new member whoever has caused the biggest fiasco of the year. Members of the government are disqualified, to stop it becoming just another aspect of the cabinet.

14 May 1993

A Knight of Splendour

MY FATHER, WHO was a civil servant, was knighted in 1947, and I got the morning off school to go to Buckingham Palace for the ceremony. Laurence Olivier was in the same group, but differed from the others because they had never been knighted before, whereas he had, often – indeed perhaps twice a day on matinée days. He therefore knew how to do the thing properly. We sat and watched while a man from the Ministry of Pensions shuffled forward, ducked his head in the way he had been told, and was tapped on the shoulder by the King, to be followed by an Air Marshall for the same treatment. When it came to Sir Laurence's turn his name was called but nothing happened, until we all looked round to see what was up, and then, and not before, he swept down the aisle and flung himself upon one knee before his sovereign, with a grand theatrical gesture as if he was being dubbed Knight on the field of Agincourt. The King looked as if he thought this pretty odd, and seemed almost on the point of giggling, as well he might because Sir Laurence had also bleached his hair and had a peculiar haircut, which I suppose was meant to make him look Danish, for purposes of filming Hamlet.

My father's knighthood had a greater effect upon my mother than on him. It coincided with her sudden conversion to radical socialism which she practiced in Wisborough Green, in the heart of Sussex and also in the constituency with the largest Tory majority in the country. She joined the Wisborough Green Labour Party, whose members were very glad to have her now she was a Lady. This may seem strange but the sitting MP was Lord Winterton, who was an Irish peer. The Wisborough Green Socialists talked incessantly about The Noble Earl, and His Lordship's support for this and that, such as his presumed support for what they called 'The Iniquitous Game Laws', such being the burning topics of the day in Wisborough Green, or at least among the half-dozen or so Socialists to be found there. When my mother joined them they were very pleased because they felt that in Her Ladyship they now had a court card of their own, which they could play right back at His Lordship, though of course they had a false estimation of the value of the wife of a knight-bachelor as against an Irish peer.

I once accompanied my mother and some of the brotherhood to one of Lord Winterton's meetings during an election campaign. The high spot of the evening was when His Lordship gave a neat answer to a hostile political question. I do not remember the question, but I shall never forget the answer, which was: 'Take your hands out of your pockets when you speak to me!' It was an answer which, had I been a floating voter, would have made me a lifelong Tory.

Before her conversion to Socialism my mother's main interest was in English Literature, which she always pronounced with a capital L. She now combined English Literature and Socialism. The entire membership of the Wisborough Green Labour Party would fit into the dining room of our house (which was known as 'Her Ladyship's country residence') without the need for extra chairs, and they took to doing so. She formed them into a discussion group which, drawing on Gray's *Elegy*, she christened 'The Village Hampdens'.

The literary reference was lost upon them, but they took the idea on trust, and said how much they appreciated the revival of the fine old English custom of 'having a hampden', and would frequently assemble to oppose with dauntless breast His Lordship and the iniquitous game laws. I told my mother that she had struck a rich vein with the Hampdens, and it could be further developed with a poetry society called the 'Mute Miltons', the Home Guard re-named the 'Guiltless Cromwells', and a choral society called the 'Noiseless Tenors'.

28 May 1993

Only Zombies Need Apply

MY ELDEST DAUGHTER is looking for a job, so I read through the Appointments part of the *Times* recently, instead of throwing it away as usual. It came as rather a shock to find that even if I were 30 years younger I should be unemployable. Leaving aside such matters as lack of ability or defects of character, there seems to be almost no demand for human beings. Individuals with extraordinary collections of strange talents cannot possibly exist in the numbers being advertised for, so British industry must be run by something else. At a guess I would say it was zombies made by transplant surgeons out of people killed on motorways.

The rule when advertising for zombies is 'throw grammar and syntax to the winds, and use dots instead of words'. 'Board level player with the very highest profile in their field' goes near the top of an advert, and 'Expanding presence in key global markets' lower down. There is, I suppose, a sort of general implication that the one is searching for the other.

Language appropriate to people will no longer do. Zombies are not graduates, they are 'graduate calibre'. For a 'to £75,000 package' zombie they want '● Graduate calibre'. For a 'Managing Director Consumer Durables' they want another style of zombie with another shape of dot, viz., '◆ Graduate calibre'. I think the different dots indicate a different calibre – a small bore in one case, but a large bore in the other, or perhaps a smooth bore rather than a round bore.

A lot of zombies are currently employed in making blue chips. 'May be from blue chip industry' they say, or 'Blue chip background desirable'. The game in which the chips are used is not revealed, though some advertisers declare themselves to be 'major players'. They want their zombies to be 'team players', so they must be like those Argentinian polo players, known as hired assassins, who are brought in to strengthen the side – which in the case of zombies is otherwise made up of low-handicap humans. I think some world-wide poker game is in progress in which several participants propose to cheat by making their own blue chips, so the zombies need to be able to run fast to get out of trouble, which is why everyone is always interested in their track records.

In one case all the zombies are joined together and 'operate as a seamless part of one of the world's leading firms'. This should keep them from molesting the secretaries, which you would think might be a problem with the 'bottom line focused leader... with hands-on approach and eye for detail'. This one is wanted by some people called FMCG, a name you cannot pronounce as it has no vowels, so possibly zombies communicate in grunts and go around saying 'fmcg, fmcg' to each other.

Sometimes the zombies are addressed directly with confident remarks about the future, such as 'You will be in your early 30s'. This seems an obvious thing to say to a zombie of twenty-nine which it only requires the passage of time to bring about. I think it shows that older zombies can be re-worked and is intended to convey to zombies of forty-five that their new employer will fit them with re-conditioned engines.

If kept in a nice dry cave these arcane documents would serve to puzzle papyrologists in 2,000 years time. Meanwhile my nightmare is that by some dreadful mistake I might get one of their jobs. Having passed myself off as one whose skills lay in driving targeted key direct-response mechanisms in a recession-proof niche market, I might sit down to lunch between a primary interface with an excellent knowledge of fixed income derivatives and a high-profile deal maker with extensive Power-House skills on multiple platforms. Whatever should we talk about?

11 June 1993

Going Over Budget

I HAVE BEEN trying to strike out on a new career as a fearless investigative journalist. I was led into this by an advertisement in the *Sunday Telegraph* which said I could hire a Ford Fiesta for £149 per week 'through any of our participating rental locations in the UK'. So I rang the number they gave and the conversation went like this:

Voice: This is Budget Rent-a-car, Denise speaking, how can I help you?

E: Ah, Denise, how kind! You can help me by telling me how much it will cost to hire a Ford Fiesta in Glasgow for eight days, starting on 18th May.

Denise: What location?

E: Glasgow.

Denise: What vehicle?

E: Ford Fiesta.

Denise: What date?

E: 18th May.

Denise: What period?

E: Eight days.

Denise: £190 per week.

E: But Denise, can you tell me why I am looking at an advertisement which says £149 per week all inclusive?

Denise: (accusingly) You did not mention that!

E: I am mentioning it now.

Denise: Hold on. (Pause) I have checked with the computer and that is only on offer in London.

It did not seem that Denise's idea of helping me would get me any further, and I feared to ask for a moron in the higher echelons in case I lost my temper, so I brought the conversation to a close.

As well as vowing never to rent a Budget car in any circumstances whatever, I sent the advertisement to the Trading Standards Officer in the hope that he would send the Budget gang to Botany Bay in chains. If any more advertisements appeared I would know that the culprits had passed through the hands of Group Four Security and escaped as usual.

Then I thought I should not give up yet, so I rang the number again (it was a freephone) and this time it went like this:

Voice: This is Budget Rent-a-car, Margaret speaking, how can I help you?

E: Ah, Margaret, I am much obliged! You can help by telling me the name of your managing director.

Margaret: We do not have one. We have a President.

E: I am not at all surprised. Who is he?

Margaret: He is H Luckweld and he lives in Hemel Hempstead.

Then she rattled off his address like one o' clock, and as she had it at her fingertips, I think that angry people must be ringing up for H all the time. I wrote and told H that I was a fearless investigative journalist about to expose him between the covers of *The Oldie* as a cheat and charlatan who said things could be had in any participating location when what he meant was London. Naturally I thought he would instantly begin to tremble and ring me up with offers of chauffeur-driven limousines at no cost to myself for as long as I liked. To this I would scornfully reply that I was not to be bribed out of my relentless quest for the truth, and that it was proper journalistic behaviour for me to seek his side of the story.

All I got was a brush off, four weeks later, from Customer Relations (UK and Intl) so I was brought up short in my new career, wondering what investigative journalists do when nobody takes a blind bit of notice of them. I must ask Paul Foot next time we meet, as I expect he knows.

Worst of all, I ended up with a Budget car anyway. I booked with people called Holiday Autos, but they turned out to be a front organisation for Budget, so it was a Budget girl who tried to extort an extra day's rental for the car although I had paid in full. If this column comes to an abrupt end it will be because I am in hospital with my legs broken by Budget heavies sent to collect this undue debt. Investigative journalism is a tough life, but one must remain fearless, even if unsuccessful.

25 June 1993

Je Ne Comprends Pa

ONE OF THE young ladies at *The Oldie* has written me a letter saying, 'I have the software to cope – even if you are not sure what software is.' Of course I am sure what software is. It is the opposite of hardware, which is American for ironmongery. If you rode down one of those long dusty streets on a horse the signs said Hardware, Software, Saloon, Bank and Guns. At the software store you bought your shirts and writing paper, sometimes known as 'dry goods'. Her letter was about some ironmongery called a scanner, and if she had said 'I have the dry goods to cope' I should have understood equally well. She means that if the scanner breaks down she has a boiler suit and a baseball cap so she will not get covered in oil while she fixes it. It is amazing what ignorance the young attribute to the old.

Young Gunning

I am always being exhorted by young people to 'take care'. This is not due to any particular anxiety that at my age I should do my kerb drill when crossing the road, or take a firm grip on the bannisters when coming downstairs, as they say it to each other all the time. They always part with the words 'Take care', as if they lived their lives in a state of constant precaution. In rather the same way they close their otherwise interminable telephone calls with the words 'Speak to you soon!' This is to give notice that having drained the conversation to the dregs they propose to retire, refuel and recharge before starting another telephone marathon, preferably at somebody else's expense.

I regard these as fairly harmless foibles, but when I mentioned them to a young person of my acquaintance I was surprised to have retorted upon me with some venom a few characteristics of oldies which I had always thought of as quite innocent.

'They go,' she said, 'to the post office at lunch time. They have the whole day in which to go to the post office as they have long since ceased to do any work or be anything other than a drain upon society, but they go at lunch time in order to delay those of us who are in a hurry. When they arrive at the counter they buy two stamps and say to the person at the window "I'm eighty-two, you know," in order to hold things up still further.'

Yes, I recognise the picture, and now see why so many oldies shun the cash dispensers in the bank and go for the cashiers instead. There is no point in telling a cash dispenser you are eighty-two, but the cashiers are paid to listen and one should get as much out of one's bank as one can. Also the other people waiting for the cashier are probably estate agents with large sums of money, and there is more satisfaction to be had from obstructing them than merely delaying some flibbertigibbet secretary who just wants to get five pounds out of the machine.

'Furthermore,' said my friend, now visibly warming to her theme, 'they are fiercely competitive about their operations. In fact I sometimes feel sorry for them that they only have two legs.' 'Why so?' 'Because they can only have two hip operations. Once they have got both hips in plastic the only thing they can look forward to is plastic knees, otherwise their friends will catch them up. And my father!' she added, throwing up her hands in despair. 'What, old John?' 'Old John!' she said scornfully. 'My mother and I went to Spain and left him at home, and he rang her up to ask her where she kept the Brillo pads!'

At this point my wife came zooming in out of the sun like the Red Baron. 'That is nothing to do with being old,' she said, 'it is to do with being a man.' Now that is why I do not think that women should be allowed on active service alongside men – as soon as the hard pounding starts, you find they have deserted to the enemy.

23 July 1993

Feisty FT Gets Funky

IN OUR SEARCH for a Saturday paper that does not think we want to waste the weekend reading boring articles about uninteresting people, we tried the *Financial Times*. It said that Japanese whalers are popularly portrayed as feisty fishermen; that Tutti Frutti stools come in funky colours; and that Joan Collins has chutzpah. I read somewhere that a leather-clad Marxist professor of English at Oxford is bent on destroying the language and I think he has infiltrated the FT. You have to hand it to him!

Being as ready as the next man to jump on a bandwagon as long as it is not moving too quickly, I am thinking of spearheading a movement with a new language called Inter-changeable. 'The feisty fisherman sat on the funky stool and helped himself to chutzpah'. 'Feisty Collins's tutti-frutti made the fisherman funky.' These very vivid scenes are described with words which, to me at least, are devoid of meaning and therefore a great advance on the elitist practice of requiring sense or accuracy.

This lends itself particularly well to advertising, as in the slogan: 'Feisty cats love Funky'. This can be used as a caption for anything – cats eating cat food, bond dealers drinking lager, housewives eating ice cream. You can turn it round and use the plural if you want: 'Funky cats love Feisties' for children eating potato crisps or nubile women in state-of-the-art designer jeans.

As the leather-clad professor is bound to agree that advertising copy is as worthy of serious study as Jane Eyre, I think he will be tickled more pink than he already is with my contribution to the destruction of English as the ideological apparatus of the capitalist state.

6 August 1993

The Birds

I WAS ASKED the other day if I knew anything about birds, and replied with my usual candour that this is one of many subjects on which I know almost nothing. They wanted to know about blackbirds, so I said quickly that this was a black bird with a yellow beak, as I was anxious to air what little knowledge I had. Before they could stop me I had added that the female looks like a thrush without spots on its stomach, and that further to confuse the issue blackbirds sing a lot, so that if there are thrushes and blackbirds about it is almost impossible to tell who is making the noise.

Had they not interrupted me this would have led into my short lecture on bird song, starting with an explanation that when the poet says, 'Spring, the sweet spring, pretty birds do sing: Cuckoo, jug, jug, pu we' he is supposed to be talking about a pheasant going 'jug jug' and I don't know what going 'pu we'. This would have introduced a disquisition on the futility of poets and, more particularly, writers of bird books attempting to reproduce bird song with the aid of the alphabet. There are pheasants at the bottom of our garden, but if

I went around shouting 'jug jug' they would not think I was another pheasant even if they had their eyes shut.

I would then have produced a bird book which says the thrush goes 'how-d'ye-do; Bo-peep Bo-peep; Judy Judy; pretty Dick' – whereas the blackbird has a 'musical fluting warble'. If Mr Richard Ingrams was playing a musical fluting warble on the organ and I was going 'How d'ye do, Bo-peep?' you would know which was which, but as a means of sorting out the dawn chorus it is altogether useless.

However I got no chance to make these observations because they said the matter concerned a blackbird which was bullying their cat. Every time the cat goes out it is set on by a blackbird and it is getting fed up with it. I asked whose side they were on and they said they were neutral, whereas if it had been our cat I should have been on the bird's side as our cat eats so many birds it would do it good to know what it feels like to be on the bird's end.

In my experience one blackbird looks much like another, so I said they should ask around to see if this was happening elsewhere. It might not always be the same blackbird that attacked – the blackbirds could be working on a rota. I inclined to the view that the blackbirds have formed a local branch of the Royal Society for the Protection of Birds and the first thing they are protecting themselves against is cats. Possibly all the birds are in membership, as they say in the trade union movement, but the blackbirds have been appointed as the military wing and are paid by the other birds with bits of worm.

The only other explanation I could offer was that here we had a Tom Brown among birds and theirs was a Flashman of cats, and the blackbird had decided to have it out. They pooh-poohed this and said they thought there was a nest with chicks which the blackbird was defending. This idea I regard as so banal and obvious that I am surprised that any sensible person could possibly entertain it. Much more interesting is the possibility that the worms will see what is going on and turn. If anyone sees a worm setting about a blackbird I should be glad to be informed.

20 August 1993

Money for Old Rope

I HAVE HAD a letter from a friend who went to see a play called *Rope* at the Minerva Theatre in Chichester. 'You would probably not have liked,' says she, 'the three nude men at the beginning or the amorous scene between two of them at the end.' This is not a proper use of the word 'probably', which should only be employed when there is an element of doubt. Had she said 'You would probably have tried to set the theatre on fire, or solicited contributions from the audience to buy a bomb for the purpose,' that would have been correct.

I remember *Rope* from my schooldays as a thriller about two men who murder a third to see if they can get away with it. It was suitable for schoolboys because it has no women, so none of us got soppy parts. To make the cast into naked sodomites is a sign of the diseased imagination which was once thought to be the mark of an avant-garde producer. Well, it isn't avant-garde any more, it is jolly well arrière-garde.

They ought to have been reading their newspapers, as they would have learned that almost nobody goes to the cinema any more because it is all so filthy, or watches television because it is all so beastly. Furthermore I have just read that the richest writer in history is a man called John Grisham who, says the *Telegraph*, 'doesn't write about sex, nor does he pepper his dialogue with swear words' and there are 27,745,790 copies of his novels in print. We may be reaching the end of the era, started by those idiots at Penguin, in which publishers pour out a succession of novels not fit to be printed, especially not if written by women, and most especially if the women are old enough to know better.

The literary figure whom I most admire is Lord Macaulay. His reference to a clergyman called Jeremy Collier having 'shamed the stage into something which might be called decency' sent me searching for the book in question.

Published in 1698, *A Short View of the Immorality and Profaneness of the English Stage* opens: 'Being convinced that nothing has gone farther in debauching the age than the stage-poets and play house, I thought I could not employ my time better than in writing against them.'

My sentiments entirely. He is absolutely up-to-date. Of the 'rankness and indecency of their language,' he says, 'it does in effect degrade human nature, sinks reason into appetite, and breaks down the distinction between man and beast. Goats and monkeys, if they could speak, would express their brutality in language such as this.' I believe I pioneered the fashion of not going to the cinema, having been cured of the habit by film reviews which seemed themselves to achieve the status of obscene publications. Nevertheless, without having gone there, I am sure the cinema is worse than the television, and the television abounds in what might well, could they but speak, be the outpourings of goats and monkeys. Nasty goats and monkeys, at that.

The work of Jeremy Collier is full of choice remarks like 'The more natural, the worse; for the disgust always rises with the life of the description. Offensive language, like offensive smells, does but make a man's senses a burden.' Lots of it would do for 'Voice from the Grave', and any readers who can get hold of a copy should wait till the Editor has forgotten all about it, and then send in their quotes and have the Glengoyne whisky on me.

3 September 1993

Chiz Gets on Wick

THE TIMES SAYS 'the right-on Ben Elton and Stephen Fry are about as funny as tofu', which I thought was rather severe. For those unfamiliar with the idiom, 'tofu' derives from 'totally futile' spoken in a slack-jawed manner by a young person, leaving out half the syllables as usual. If you do not think it funny for a man to put on a white coat and say 'I am a bar steward' you can describe his humour as tofu. A thing that is lamentably bad at the outset cannot go right off so it tends to go right on, as seems to have happened in this case. I cannot say myself, as I have not seen either one for five years except when taken unawares by a TV advert.

Two other words which sometimes give trouble are 'chiz' and 'theygo'. Both are words of giving and receiving much in vogue among the young. A waiter slopping a bowl of soup down on the table will say 'chiz' or 'they-go', depending on his mood. If he says 'theygo' the proper reply is 'chiz', but if he says 'chiz' the answer should be 'grike'. This is a mutation of 'great' which avoids the letter 't'. This letter is, generally speaking, anathema and thus, in a phrase such as 'got to get a better bit' all the 't's are silent. 'Chiz' may also be used on parting, to save the time and effort involved in pronouncing the word 'goodbye'.

17 September 1993

Women Studies

A PROFILE OF Prince Philip in the *Independent* not long ago blamed the troubles of the Royal Family on the headmaster of Gordonstoun, who 'never taught the boys about women. Philip's inability to pass on a sense of what women need has become increasingly stark as the two elder boys have been overtaken by marital crises'.

This sets a man searching his conscience as a father and his memory as a schoolboy. On the first count I am all right, as I often gave my son my short lecture on the subject, consisting of the one word 'Women!', spoken while casting the eyes up to heaven or some crockery to the floor. What father could do more?

The curriculum of Westminster School in the 1940s, however, was innocent of any lessons about women. I expect this was true of every public school in the country at the time, not just Westminster and Gordonstoun, so we must all be a bit strange on the subject. They may have had such lessons at Bedales or Bryanston, but these are schools for people who are strange already.

As there is nowadays an obsession for devising things to put into the National Curriculum, to be criticised by the government and taken out two years later, I have sketched out a small lesson on the subject for them to adopt as a model:

'You must always think, my dear boys, that women think exactly as men think, or you will end up in an Industrial Tribunal. The ambition of every girl is to be one of the boys, and they like you to swear, tell dirty jokes and sing rugger songs in their presence. There are certain supercilious and condescending actions such as opening doors for them, or giving up your seat to them, which should only be practised on the ones you heartily dislike. If you really want to irritate them, insist on walking on the outside of the pavement, and explain that you do this so that you and not they will be splashed by passing carriages.

'Never, never pay a woman a compliment on her appearance. Oh my juvenile friends, what is sexual harassment but a compliment gone wrong? Happily the risks in this direction are less than they used to be, as the girls generally now dress to make themselves as unattractive as yourselves. Any of you who aspire to be fashion designers have only to choose between the dingy and the bizarre to be sure of success.

'Women used to behave better than men, but this has been put a stop to. There used to be a middle ground for women between prudery and indecency, which was called modesty, but this caused inconvenience and has been abolished.*

'Women who get roles as models are now called role models, and any one of them will take her clothes off for the pleasure of the general public without the least demur. An actress of the first rank who advocates the morals of a whore is nothing out of the ordinary, which is why you get a better class of whore nowadays. You will notice that when a politician or other public figure gets mixed up with one, the whore is always much the nicer of the two.

'Blasphemy, indecency and obscenity are now approved at the highest level, and you must accept them as the common coin of female conversation among women below the age of thirty-five, or older ones who affect the manners of the young. It is a great advance on the days before the language of the barrack-room had invaded the drawing-room, and when Audrey Hepburn made films like *Breakfast at Tiffany's* with all her clothes on.

'That I think about covers the subject, and there is the bell, so you can all run along and change for mixed rugby football.'

**As Lovelace says in 'Clarissa', 'It is cruel to ask a modest women for her consent. It is creating difficulties for both.'*

1 October 1993

Salisbury – The Enfield Version

BACK IN APRIL *The Oldie* rang. Would I go to Salisbury in September to take part in the festival there? It was to be *Readings from The Oldie*, and the cast was the Editor, Miles Kington and me. September seemed a long way off so I said yes and tried to put the whole thing out of my mind.

As September crept towards us I got hold of a programme and found we were part of Literature Day. 'Literature! They think that stuff I have been sending in is Literature? They must be mad!' I rang Himself to find out the form. 'Oh I shall talk about *The Oldie*, then you and Miles will each read one of your pieces.' 'It takes five minutes to read one of my pieces.' 'Perhaps you had better bring two.'

So that was the brief, until the Friday before the Sunday when Miles Kington, whom I had never met, rang to say that the Editor had decided to go to hospital instead of coming to the show. They had rung the Festival people to see if we should cancel, but they had wailed in despair, so like the stout old troupers we are we decided that The Show Must Go On. At least I think that is what Miles decided. I was just in a panic.

The day itself can hardly be said to have dawned as there was a typhoon in progress, but perhaps the sky got a little lighter in the East. I drove to Salisbury in blinding rain, hardly able to see, and saying to myself, 'All I need now is a car crash.' I got to the pub which was the rendezvous dead on time, to find it almost deserted, so naturally I concluded that Miles Kington had had a car crash. A man with long lanky black hair turned up and I asked him if he was Miles Kington but he was not, and I did not know whether to be glad or sorry.

Miles arrived only 25 minutes late, so then we began to plan. Miles's wife was there, and she is a director of plays, so she took charge and said we should sit on either side of the Editor's empty chair and pretend we thought he was coming. It seemed a good idea but of course it did not work. We were ushered onto the stage, and there was a big black hole on the other side of the lights which seemed to have some people in it, but there were only two chairs. 'I'll get another chair,' I cried, determined to carry out instructions, and turned to find I was faced with an impenetrable wall of purple velvet, which was the curtain. As I clawed at it in an effort to find a way through, the audience obligingly laughed, and I think it was my best contribution to the show. If we ever have to do it again, with or without Himself, we must make sure that we are one chair short. I will then do my clawing-at-the-velvet act and eventually disappear, to return five minutes later, possibly through the audience, triumphantly waving a chair and crying, 'I've found one, I've found one'. It may turn out to be a trick chair which collapses under the Editor. This sort of thing is known as Literature on the Hoof.

Somehow Miles Kington steered a way through a whole hour with admirable skill. At the end some friends emerged from the black hole and said I had shown great sang-froid, which is French for when the blood runs cold with terror, so it obviously showed. Then a man from the BBC appeared, to say that he had taped it and was going to put bits of it on Radio 2, which is not a very literary place to put it.

My neighbour has a beautiful chestnut horse, and the groom told me that after a day's hunting he relives it all in his box, trembling and snorting and stamping all night. I know how he feels. As I lay in bed that night I seemed to hear Miles Kington solemnly assuring the audience that Richard Ingrams had jumped off his yacht in the Mediterranean and left a large hole in *The Oldie* pension fund, or telling an extraordinary story about a man who always went shooting with a pig in each pocket, and would have been eaten by a leper if the pigs had not saved him. This, I suppose, is Literature in the Raw.

29 October 1993

Managing Superstition

MY NEIGHBOUR, OF whom I usually have a high opinion, has played me a shabby trick. He sent me a wad of 23 letters, including one from a Dutchman who said I should send my secretary to the photocopier to make four additional copies of the whole lot, and send them to five more people. If I did I would be all right but if I broke the chain I should have bad luck.

I do not have a secretary but my wife kindly types this column for me as typing, like electric welding and pole-vaulting, is a skill I have yet to acquire.

She often objects to what I have written, and sometimes flatly refuses to type it, so whatever appears in *The Oldie* can be regarded as having got through the censor. In this case my heart quailed at her likely reaction if I asked her to go to the public library and photocopy 23 letters four times over, so I threw the whole lot in the bin, whereupon an out-of-control female solicitor rammed the back of our car and stove it in, which is bad luck if you like.

So then I dredged the letters up again and found that they are all from Captains of Industry. The fact that they are such a superstitious lot adds a new dimension to my theory of our industrial decline. I was aware that bits of British industry had fallen into the hands of foreign criminals, some of whom changed their names to Maxwell or Saunders in order to try to pass themselves off as Englishmen. If they gave the Tory party some of the money they had stolen, the Labour party said it should be given back, but if they used it to buy burial plots on the Mount of Olives nobody said anything at all. I supposed this was because the liquidators were happy to grow fat on what was left without running the risk of being liquidated themselves by Mossad for asking awkward questions.

Now I realise that those in British Industry who are not downright dishonest must be setting company policy in the light of their horoscope in the *Daily Mail*. Men who must be household names in certain households obediently send their secretaries to the photocopier and despatch these letters to other industrial nabobs with little notes saying that of course they do not believe a word of it, but just in case…

A letter apparently signed by Sir Ian MacLaurin, chairman of Tesco, sets it going with 'Sorry about this, but I am not going to break the chain.' David Jones of Next joins in, and it reaches Ken Morrison of Wm Morrison Supermarkets, who says: 'I appreciate you have better things to do – but you never quite know.' 'I concur with all the foregoing comments but why tempt providence!' says P Bailey of Peat Marwick, the celebrated liquidators. My favourite is C J Davies, the chief executive of Everest Foods, who says: 'I am very fortunate that I am not a superstitious person. However, just to be a good sport I intend to continue the chain.'

As a management technique, cultivating luck by means of chain letters is probably as effective as hiring consultants or sending the staff to business school – as it is a great deal cheaper, it makes a kind of sense. Indeed, it could even be taught at business schools; there may also be seminars for managing directors on reading tea-leaves, and on tarot cards for chief executives. There are those who say that stockmarket tipsters in the newspapers have always worked like this, but I believe they have a much better method, which is to tip all the shares there are at one time or another, and then to swank about the ones that go up and keep quiet about the ones that go down. This absolutely guarantees success.

My neighbour says he only sent me the letters to help me with my column, and I suppose in a way it has, but as the car repairs cost over £600 I have asked him not to help me any more. Also I have told the female solicitor that it is his fault about the car, in case she wants to make legal history by repudiating liability on the grounds of diminished responsibility, she being merely the helpless instrument of fate after I had thrown the letters away instead of sending them on.

12 November 1993

Belly-laughs with the Bard

IT IS A strange thing, but whenever there is a banquet in a period film everybody eats grapes and laughs all the time, and though I have been to a good many dinners in my time I have never been to one that was all grapes and giggling. This is what happens in *Much Ado About Nothing*, which I have just been to see – Emma Thompson eats a great many grapes and there is a monstrous lot of laughing at banquets.

It is one of those films which starts 10 minutes after the beginning, as there is a long bit stuck on the front to spin things out before Shakespeare has any say in what is going on. The purpose is to allow the cast to undress and have a bath, and also to giggle, which they do on the way to the bath as well as when eating. This sets the bard back a bit and it is some time before he can claw his way into the action and persuade you that it is not going to be as stupid as the beginning suggests. It only cost £2.20 to see it in Brighton and I suppose the nudity-in-the-bath (plus the copulation-on-the-balcony which they have shoved in in violation of the text) can be described as cheap thrills for those who like that sort of thing.

Apart from that it is all right. In fact it is more than all right, it is superb,

and if you could contrive to arrive 10 minutes late and be busy unwrapping a toffee during the balcony scene there is no reason why you should not enjoy it immensely. Emma Thompson, Richard Briers and Kenneth Branagh speak all the lines so that you know what they mean and all the jokes so that they are funny. There is a sort of technicolour Don Pedro, the part being played by a black man in phosphorescent blue jeans, but he too is all right and I see the point that black actors should be allowed parts other than Othello.

But it is not wholly free from the standard faults of Shakespeare productions, and musing on it all I have evolved two rules for the guidance of actors which I shall put forward when asked to be Visiting Professor at RADA, an invitation I am expecting any minute.

Rule One: Actors should not conduct themselves like football players.

Whatever they may do off the stage, when on it actors should behave as if they were normal. I appreciate that it will be difficult for many of them, but the fact is that normal men shake hands in public but otherwise do not touch each other unless engaged in manly sports. Therefore all pawing, hugging, embracing and walking around arm-in-arm should be excluded unless strictly required by the text. This may spoil the fun for the actors but they are supposed to be performing for our benefit, not theirs.

Rule Two: Leave the laughing to the audience.

The drama class should spend days, if not weeks, discussing and practising the following quote from Lord Chesterfield: 'Having mentioned laughing, I must particularly warn you against it. In my mind there is nothing so illiberal or ill-bred as audible laughter. I am neither of a melancholy nor of a cynical disposition; and am as willing and as apt to be pleased as anybody; but I am sure that since I have had the full use of my reason nobody has ever heard me laugh.'

Actors commonly laugh for no purpose or for the wrong purpose, which is to signal to the audience that a joke is intended. I saw a production of *The Way of the World* in which one actor after another made the rest of the cast hoot with laughter, while the rest of us stared glumly up, wondering what the joke was. Maggie Smith, on the other hand, did not laugh at all but reduced the audience to tears of merriment by the way she spoke the lines. Actors who haven't the knack of making jokes funny should either get jobs as bus conductors, which gives them a chance to practise, or as television comedians, where it is not required.

26 November 1993

A Welcome Stranger

A YEAR AGO I wrote in rather a gloomy way about the prospect of Christmas, and now it is looming up again. At the last count there are going to be 10 people in the house, and I need to get the septic tank emptied before they arrive. However there is a glimmer of hope, because one of them is Mick. Mick came last year and furthermore when we went on holiday to Cyprus Bethan came too. The point about Mick and Bethan is that they are not our children, they are someone else's, and they seem to have a good effect on the Enfields.

I mentioned this to a friend who is one of five children and has accumulated four on his own account. 'Oh yes,' he said, 'whenever you go on a family holiday you must always take a stranger.' He threw this out as if it were common knowledge, but it has taken me 64 years to discover. From what I make out the stranger acts as a sort of lightning conductor, earthing the tension when the atmosphere becomes over-charged, which is usually pretty often. My only worry is that Mick has been my daughter's boyfriend for some time so we might start to regard him as one of the family, in which case he would not work and I don't see how I could get him reconditioned.

There ought to be a way of arranging a swap, like one of those computer-based dating arrangements, with a bank of suitable young people for loan or exchange to leaven the lump of family occasions. They would need to be matched to the families with care or it could turn out like an unsuccessful French exchange, when you get one that is brilliant at tennis when all yours are hopeless. I suppose it might be necessary to interview the candidates, so this should not be undertaken as a commercial venture by anyone with too strong an antipathy to young people. But apart from that I don't see a difficulty.

Pop Calling the Kettle Back

One Christmas my wife said she wanted an electric kettle. It wasn't a very exciting present but I got it and gave it to her from the cat or the goldfish, I forget which. After six weeks it stopped working so I took it back to the shop. 'We will send it away,' they said, 'come back in three weeks.'

'But how are we to manage without a kettle for three weeks?'

Shrug. Shrug. 'Come back in three weeks.'

I rang the Trading Standards Officer and he said they were within their rights, so I waited three weeks and went back. 'It hasn't come in,' they said. 'Give it another week.' Now it happened that in my office there was a temporary secretary who had lived for some years in America and was, I think, Jewish. I told her the story and she said, 'I know what you will do. You will go in and they will say, "It's not ready – OK?", and you will say, "Sorry to have bothered you", and slink out.'

This had a ring of truth so I asked what I ought to do and she gave me a crash course in Jewish American consumer behaviour. I must embarrass them as much as possible; I must make sure everyone in the shop was looking at me; I must shout, bang the counter, stamp up and down, and make it abundantly plain that I was getting rotten service from this lousy shop.

Such behaviour is foreign to my mild disposition, but I had asked for advice and felt obliged to follow it, so I worked myself into a suitable rage as I walked to the shop and strode boldly to the counter. It was not ready and I forget what I said but at the first shot the man capitulated, fled to the storeroom, ran back and pressed upon me a brand new kettle, so I was left bouncing about on the balls of my feet with no one to hit, like a boxer who has trained to go 12 rounds but knocked his man out in 30 seconds. Still, I had a new kettle and I took it home and told the children all about it, thinking they would be impressed with me. They weren't, of course. 'How awful,' they said. 'We can't bear people who behave like that in shops.'

10 December 1993

Funny Money

THE TORIES USED to have a much better economic policy than the present one, and it was called Stop-Go. When we were having a Stop Mr Harold Macmillan came on the television and said: 'It's no good writing a cheque for a guinea when you've only got a pound in the bank.'

At the time only a small proportion of the populace had bank accounts and the only people who still dealt in guineas were racehorse auctioneers, but all the people who never wrote cheques or bought racehorses understood quite well that this was a Stop. When Mr Macmillan told us we had never had it so good this meant that we were having a Go, and all of us always knew exactly where we were.

By contrast the current policy is impossible to follow. There used to be strident demands that we should save our money, and this was called the Victorian Value of Thrift. Then we were told to get out and spend it whether we had it or not, and this was called Show Confidence in the Economy. Then they went quiet and said nothing and I did not like the sound of that at all. I was right, because by the time this piece appears the Chancellor will have come clean and said he is going to take it away from us, and that is called Reducing the Fifty Billion Deficit.

Harold Macmillan was the most prescient of economists, correctly forecasting the Fifty Billion Deficit by pointing out that you cannot live for ever on the sale proceeds of the family silver. I am sure that if asked he would have said 'It's no good saying you're having a Go if you're really having a Stop', but something very like that seems to be going on at present. It could be called the Horatian Principle, because it resembles the scene in *Horatius* when 'those behind cried "Forward!" and those before cried "Back!" '. The Prime Minister behind keeps telling us it's a Go, while the Chancellor before cries 'Stop'.

They manage these things much better in Turkish Cyprus. The editor of *The Oldie* has done me several good turns, including paying me handsomely so that I can afford to go there, and accepting an advertisement from Kyrenia Villa Contacts so that I got a good place to stay. Once there we found that they have a way of dealing with galloping inflation, which is quite the best thing of its kind that I have come across. They give the tourists more and more money for their currency, and they leave their own prices alone.

They fixed the entrance fee to Kyrenia Castle at 5,000 lire when this was worth having, and then forgot about it, so now the man takes 25p off you before he lets you in. They were giving out 19,000 lire to the pound, which my wife spotted was near enough 1,000 to the shilling, so we went back to thinking in Olde English money and she came back from the grocer having bought two loaves of bread, two rolls of lavatory paper and a bunch of grapes for 17/6d. Mr Major should hire as many villas as are needed to house the whole cabinet and send them there for lessons in political economy, as everybody seemed to be entirely happy with the arrangement, and it is perfectly easy to understand.

24 December 1993

A Board-Line Case

A SINGER CALLED George Michael is trying to get out of his contract with Sony, and the key precedent is a 1901 case called *Mr Ellistrim* vs *the Ballymacelligott Co-operative Agricultural and Dairy Society*. Who'd have thought a small Irish farmer could help a multi-millionaire pop star?

I once studied law by correspondence. Circumstantial evidence, they said, can be after the event, as when an offer of marriage to an unmarried mother was allowed as evidence of paternity. I could understand the principle, but the case was called *Owen* vs *The Powell Duffryn Steam Coal Company*. Whatever happened? Did the unhappy Owen enter the boardroom with a tea-tray, to be set upon by the entire board, one of whom later made honourable amends with an offer of marriage? I never found out ...

7 January 1994

Hollywood Beckons

MUCH TO OUR delight the Sainsbury superstore outside Chichester has burned to the ground. There are those who say that this is because it was built of expanded polystyrene and sited on an old rubbish tip giving off methane gas, but this has been strongly denied. Quite right too, as it is a most facile explanation, and I prefer to think that it is a judgement on them for defacing a cathedral city with such a hideous building and then opening the beastly thing on Sundays.

Our windows are being painted by a volunteer fireman who says that as his Appliance was weaving its way through Chichester late that night all the surviving small shop-keepers had opened up. They were doing a brisk trade, rejoicing in the temporary discomfiture of the ogre that had threatened to destroy them. Good luck to them. The Tory Party believes in small businesses, and the Almighty even more so, it seems.

Since then the river Lavant has flooded and a lot of Chichester is under water, which further confirms my theory. 'With Fear and Horrour shook the guilty World / Lest Pyrrha's Age return…' (Horace, *Odes* 1.2, translation Francis). And 'Pyrrha's Age' is another flood like Noah's. So you see, they should have kept Sunday special.

I think there may be material for a film here, especially as there is a lot of unsavoury money to be had by distorting the truth for the benefit of the American market. In my script, when Sainsbury's bursts into flames the brutal and licentious Sussex Constabulary will decide it is a case of IRA arson and arrest three fleeing shoppers at random. A pregnant woman, an old-age pensioner and an Irishman in a wheel-chair will be ruthlessly tortured till they confess, and then be locked up on life sentences. Fifteen years later they get let out by a corrupt judge played by Ian Richardson, who is being blackmailed by an Afro-Caribbean barrister played by Emma Thompson with a black face.

This gives an acceptable picture of British justice and should go down well with Noraid. The only snag is that they have already made a film called *In the Name of the Father* which appeals to the same audience and which, says the *Telegraph*, 'takes great liberties with factual accuracy'. The producer, Mr Jim Sheridan, says it is 'a dramatic interpretation of the truth' and so is mine, and he did not think of giving Emma Thompson a black face, so mine has a bit extra going for it.

21 January 1994

Marred Marriages

THE OTHER NIGHT my wife was out and my neighbour's wife was away, so he cooked us a bachelor meal. Late in the evening I said to him sententiously: 'When I look back on my life I realise that I have done a great deal of harm to a great many marriages.' Not unreasonably this caused him some alarm, as the last thing he wanted was to be burdened with my embarrassing confidences. 'In fact,' I went on, 'the number of wives that I have seduced from their marital duty is really very high.'

I could see that he was now extremely uncomfortable, as who would not be in such circumstances? 'I have done it,' I said, 'simply by saying "I do not like sailing." If I said "I am going sailing in the Greek islands" everyone would say "How lovely!", but it is not lovely. The Greek islands are the least interesting parts of Greece, and the worst way to see them is by yacht. As everyone knows that has tried it, the living conditions are cramped, and the sailing itself is either dull or dangerous.

'Now there are a great many men with yachts who have never stopped to ask whether their wives like it, and the women have buried the question deep in their sub-conscious minds and never faced it. When I come along and have my say, I take the lid off. Women who have been married for years to retired naval commanders with boats at Bosham now realise that they hate boats and loathe sailing. They won't do it any more. This leaves the husband bereft of crew and enjoyment of what he has always deemed to be his conjugal rights.'

'In me,' I said, 'you are looking at the rock on which a great many marriages have foundered.' My neighbour looked very relieved that I had not said what he thought I was going to say.

4 February 1994

Declining Tankards

THE TROUBLE WITH a Golden Age is that you do not realise it is one until it is over. People did not go about saying, 'This is a Golden Age – isn't it lovely?'; they said, 'Oh damn, the post is late!' or 'Oh hell, it's raining!' just as they do now. But looking back from the Leaden Age in which we live through the intervening Bronze and Silver Ages, I can see that civilisation in this country peaked in 1950 and that was a Golden Age.

You can see it by listing the things that we did not have, such as drugs, litter, computer games, video nasties, foul films, obscene theatre, traffic jams, muzak, people sleeping on streets, impenetrable packaging, aggressive beggars, supermarkets and motorways, to name but a few. We did, on the other hand, have good public transport, a literate BBC, and far less vulgar newspapers, and people did not panic if their child went out of sight in a public park.

'Ah,' say those who were not there, 'but you had rationing.' So we did, and the nation was better fed than it ever was before or since. There was even a certain amount of fun to rationing. My mother went into the butcher's shop in Petworth and asked for the two chops that her ration books entitled her to. Then she said, 'It is not very nice weather.' 'Madam,' said the butcher severely, 'we must take the weather that God sends to us.'

'Ah yes,' said my mother, 'but His ways are not always our ways.' 'Madam, that is very true,' said the butcher, and gave her four chops. So she came home in triumph, having got twice the ration by her skill in repartee. Nowadays you can have two chops or four chops or even eight chops, and the whole thing has been totally de-skilled.

'Ah,' say those again who were not there, 'but the women were downtrodden.' Perhaps they were, but it did not seem to show very much. Shirley Williams and Lady Thatcher have never struck me as downtrodden and any efforts I have made at downtreading my wife have been conspicuous failures.

In 1950 I was at Oxford. If you wanted a pint of beer in hall you caught the eye of a scout, who brought it to you in a silver tankard dating back, I do believe, to 1660. (They had loyally melted down the earlier ones and given the silver to Charles I.) I dined there again not long ago and observed that those who wanted beer had to carry it into hall in a glass tankard from the cellar. There were no scouts to give it to them. You might think that if you put a silver tankard into the hands of a modern undergraduate he or she would pocket it, as likely as not. You might think that, and whether you do or not, there must somewhere be a vault full of silver tankards which cannot be used for the purpose for which they were intended, namely for undergraduates to drink from.

'Ah,' say those who were not there, 'but it is much nicer for those who would previously have been scouts. Instead of waiting on people like you they are now… ' and there they falter, as they realise the word they are searching for is 'unemployed'.

Quite Sufficient

The time has now come to say Enough is Enough about saying 'Enough is Enough'. Everybody is always saying Enough is Enough even when nil is the right amount, as in: 'We must say to the bombers, the murderers and the rapists "Enough is Enough!" '

The phrase is particularly popular with trades union speechmakers, who regard it as a sure-fire conclusion to a rousing peroration. All the head Boilermaker need say is: 'It is time to say to the government / employers / management "Enough is Enough!" ' and all the other boilermakers rise and cheer. The phrase has such a hold on the nation that I expect one day to find Macbeth capering about the stage waving his sword and shouting: 'Lay on Macduff, / And damn'd be him that first cries, Hold, enough is enough!'

18 February 1994

Thanks, But No Thanks

One of the pleasures of getting older and older is that one cares less and less about more and more. I never wanted a Lagonda, a Rolex or a yacht, but now I also do not want a racehorse or a house in the Dordogne. I do not want a holiday in the Carribean as there is always a frightful noise and nothing to do but sit on sand. For lots of money I could get a grey vest, white shirt, woman's cardigan, ill-fitting blue jacket and a pull-over to tie round my waist, and if I put them all on and did not shave for three days I should look like the male model in the *Times*, or a tramp, and I don't want to do that either.

Going without things I do not want has become a constant source of virtuous entertainment, and if I were a reformed alcoholic I should spend a lot of time looking in the windows of off-licences. It was in this frame of mind that I was at Victoria station having an innocent and peaceful time wandering through the shops looking at all the things I did not want. It became a sort of litany: 'I do not want any patterned socks. I do not want any jockey briefs.' Then into W H Smith: 'I do not want the *Farmers' Weekly*. I do not want any Jilly Cooper.'

Then suddenly: 'Hallo, here is a lady sitting at a desk who wants £2 and my signature. She says she will analyse my character. But if I give her my signature it will be easy for her to forge it. Is she that sort of person? Perhaps I need to analyse her character. Anyway I know quite enough about my own character to be going on with. But consumer spending helps the economy. Green shoots! Should I give her £2 and sign "David Mellor" or "Alan Clarke"?'

I did not. I wandered on, chanting softly to myself, rather like Pooh Bear, 'I do not want to give away my signature. I do not want my character analysed.' Then suddenly: 'Chocolates!'

Now that was serious. When it comes to chocolate I can take it or leave it alone, but if my wife had to choose between me and chocolates, she would choose chocolates. They were Belgian chocolates which was bad. Or rather, it was good, because she loves Belgian chocolates, but it was bad because they came from Belgium. Buying chocolate is good for the Third World, but buying Belgian chocolates is bad for the balance of payments. Well, it was only a small hole in the trade figures; I bought ten and they cost £4.

Then it hit me! Just as the girl finished sealing up the chocolates I realised: 'It is Lent! My wife will not eat these chocolates until Easter, which is weeks away. What am I to do? Shall I have my character analysed twice, and pay in chocolates? No, I want to meet someone nice to whom I can give them. To whom would I like to give my chocolates? Joanna Lumley! Where are you, Joanna Lumley? I want to give you £4 worth of Belgian chocolates. She is not here. I wish it was *The Oldie* luncheon, then I could go around giving chocolates to famous people.'

But the final solution to the chocolate problem was that I forgot them on the train and I expect they were blown up by mistake for a bomb. As Kai Lung might have said, 'It is unwise for one of a forgetful turn of mind to place the Emperor's jewels upon the luggage rack of a river boat.'

A further point I wish to make is that my column has at different times been called cantankerous and even curmudgeonly, but it will be seen that on this occasion my thoughts were all directed towards the good of humanity, the benefit of the economy, the proper observation of religious festivals, and giving harmless pleasure to my family and people whom I admire at a distance. It is not right to call a man of such an amiable disposition cantankerous just because he gets irritated by foul-mouthed comedians, pornographic novelists, Andy Warhol, Dennis Potter, and a few other things. 'Right-minded' would seem a better adjective.

4 March 1994

Famous Old Members

I DO MOST devoutly hope that the Master and Fellows of University College Oxford will not put up a statue of Bill Clinton with no clothes on. 'Why ever should they?' you may ask.

Not because Hillary has stolen his trousers, nor in reference to any possible marital peccadilloes, but because their predecessors did of Shelley who was at that college, as was Bill Clinton, and as was I. Shelley was only there for six months before they threw him out and while Bill Clinton lasted longer, the college did not think anything of him either at the time. After Shelley had become a famous dead poet they put up a staring white monument of such anatomical detail as to bring a blush to the cheek of a young person, and representing him as having been drowned and his clothes fallen off in the process. As he was weltering in the deep for fifteen days before they fished him out he cannot have looked like that at all, and I think they just did it because they felt like it.

I hope they won't feel like it about Bill. He sauntered away a couple of years at Oxford and left, like Shelley, without a degree. In a recent issue of the

College Record the authorities called Shelley 'our most famous old member' (which is a bit like calling Guy Fawkes 'our most famous parliamentarian'), but now B C is who he is, this may no longer stand. Certainly they are very keen on him, overlooking his obvious faults such as that his eyes are much too small, and I fear a statue may be in the offing.

In order to head off anything in the nudity line, I wish to offer a suggestion which would establish him as an international statesman rather than an emperor with no clothes, and make it appropriate to dress him accordingly. He told us in his helpful way, during the Presidential elections, how to solve the problems of Northern Ireland. Two of the Kennedy brothers used to offer similar kind advice when they were alive, and the one who is still alive still does.

Also they send other Kennedys along to smooth the path of British justice by turning up in our courts, and Bill obligingly shows us the proper way to handle Gerry Adams. They do this out of the goodness of their hearts and any suggestion that they are just after the Noraid vote is unworthy. Certainly no Univ man would stoop to such a thing, not even to turn attention from his financial difficulties.

Now it has been my experience over a long working life that it is no earthly use having the solution in one place and the problem in another – the trick is to bring the two together. I really think the best thing would be, Bill Clinton having got the solution, to give him the problem to go with it and make a present of Northern Ireland to America.

There is not the least geographical or administrative difficulty in this idea. The distance from Washington to Belfast is less than the distance from Washington to Honolulu, and as they manage very well with Hawaii as the 50th state of the Union, they could do just as well with Ulster as the 51st. For solving the problem Bill Clinton would get the Nobel Peace Prize which would save him from the sticky end for which, like Shelley, he seems to be heading, and would make it appropriate to do the statue as a Roman senator in toga and sandals. If anything has to be left off, let it be the sandals.

15 April 1994

Patients Are Their Own Reward

MY LATEST ATTEMPT at investigative journalism nearly came to grief owing to my being scooped by Auberon Waugh. I was working undercover in a wig and dark glasses to expose a shocking scandal in the Health Service when he blew the whole thing wide open in the *Telegraph*. In his case it was a letter delivered to his house from a group of doctors and addressed to a lady who had not lived there for 38 years. In mine it was a letter from some other doctors summoning my mother for a health check although she has been dead for 40 years.

Being an experienced local government officer I knew, as I thought, what to do. I approached the District Auditor and asked who audited these doctors. 'Coopers and Lybrand,' he said, and gave me the name of the man to write to. So I wrote, in October last, and told him all about it. In January 1994 I wrote again (investigative journalism is quite a leisurely business, I find) to ask why I had had no reply. I got an answer this time saying there was no trace of my first letter, but that I should write to the West Sussex Family Health Service Authority.

This seemed like passing a message from the gamekeeper to the poacher via the landowner but I rang the WSFHSA, disguising my voice in a rich Brummy accent à la Forgan, and asked if they had any system of internal audit. 'No,' they said, 'Coopers and Lybrand do it for us.'

‘And is it right that the more patients a doctor has, the more money he gets?’

‘Yes,’ they said.

‘So,’ thinks I, ‘this is one for the Secretary of State,’ and I sent the correspondence to La Belle Bottomley pointing out that while she has been critical of grey suits in the health service who didn’t do much for their money, there seemed to be some similarly-clad auditors with the same outlook on life, and perhaps she should look into it.

Mrs B sent my letter to Leeds, from where a lady whose title is Corporate Affairs Intelligence Unit wrote to say she had written to the WSFHSA Chief Executive, one Terry Knott, telling him to write to me, which he never did. I had given the Coopers and Lybrand man a copy of my letter to Mrs B, and he now chimed in to say that whatever they said at the WSFHSA they did have a system of internal audit so it was their affair, not his. I wrote to the silent Terry Knott to ask if he agreed, to which he did not reply.

A lady who said she was the Chairman of the WSFHSA then rang to say they had internal auditors and they are called Price Waterhouse but they do not like to send for them as they ‘cost thousands’. They themselves ‘have no right to go in and sort through doctors’ lists as the doctors are very sensitive about patient confidentiality’. They do, however, discuss matters with the ‘Primary Health Care Team’ which I think means the doctor’s secretary.

She agreed that the doctors in question had probably been drawing a fee for my mother for the last 40 years, but said things were much worse in London. (This was meant to be consoling, as when they say we need not worry about falling standards in public life in this country as things are much worse in Italy.)

Possibly an epidemic of Mad Doctor Disease has broken out in Somerset and Sussex, having been rife in London for a long time. The symptoms are that doctors accumulate hallucinatory patients whom they long to examine but can never get their hands on, although their existence is proved by the fact that each one is productive of money. Having observed that farmers get paid for doing nothing to 15 per cent of the land, Mrs B must have ruled that doctors may treat, or rather not treat, 15 per cent of their patients likewise. The only way to be certain that they never turn up at the surgery is to make sure that they are dead, and I suspect that nowadays 15 per cent of all patients are defunct.

29 April 1994

Stomping and Sledging

ALMOST MY ONLY interest in sport nowadays is in watching Englishmen beating foreigners and I do not get too much chance to indulge it. Wimbledon has been quite useless since the year Virginia Wade won the women's finals; it is a waste of time watching a couple of foul-mouthed foreigners bashing a ball about on Centre Court. On the other hand, if six identical-looking men in bathing caps are swimming 100 yards by the utterly boring breast-stroke, I only need to be told that one is an Englishman with a chance of a gold medal and I am riveted to the TV set.

Whenever we do something like getting knocked out of the World Cup there is a lot of breast-beating and talk of improving the standard of play but we really need to improve the standard of cheating. The Australians cheat at cricket and the New Zealanders at rugby, for which they offer the strange antipodean excuse that it ought to be all right over here as they do it all the time down-under. This is as if a cannibal said he ought to be allowed to eat people in England as it is the regular thing in New Guinea's jungles.

Accepting that it is futile to expect sporting occasions to be occasions for sportsmanship, the All Blacks could be dealt with by reviving the Anglo-Saxon all-male dance called the fyrbrd, in which the idea is to trip your partner and stamp on his face. While the New Zealanders were jumping in the air and sticking their tongues out in that thing they call the Hakka (or something) our men could be tripping them up and stamping on their faces, which should ensure that the game is won before it starts. When it comes to cricket we need a latter-day Barnes Wallis to improve on the Pakistani technique of doctoring the ball, so that it describes a figure of eight or takes a serpentine course on its way from bowler to batsman.

The Australian method of cheating is called sledging, and not tobogganning as I thought before, and this is a job for M16. If they could provide a photograph of the batsman's wife in bed with the wicket-keeper – preferably the English wicket-keeper but if necessary the Australian one – this, if slipped to the batsman between overs, should unsettle him enough to get him out, especially if the ball is coming at him like a snake.

In the matter of umpiring a lot can be learned from the commanding officer of the regiment in which I did my national service. His way of

umpiring the sergeants v officers cricket match was always to give the officers out and never to give the sergeants out, which produced universal satisfaction as the sergeants liked winning and it made the officers laugh. If this principle were extended to test cricket and umpires always gave foreigners out and never gave Englishmen out it would do more for national morale than any number of General Agreements on Tariffs and Trade, and give me endless hours of harmless pleasure.

10 June 1994

Fantasy Island

I READ THAT it is everyone's daydream to be on Desert Island Discs. I had not thought of daydreaming about that, but I tried it and found it very agreeable. I particularly like the reverential way in which Miss Lawley addressed me, saying things like 'And then you went to school?' and making it sound as if I had won the Victoria Cross. I think it goes like this:

SL: What do you want for your first record?

EE: Do I have to have a damned gramophone on this island? I'd much rather have a mountain bike.

SL: I'm afraid you do.

EE: Oh well, when I was eight they sent me to prep school where they made us sing a hymn every night. I'll have 'The Day Thou Gavest' to remind me how nice it is to be on a desert island instead of banged up in a pre-school dormitory.

(Music)

SL: In the war you were sent to Canada. That must have given you a great sense of achievement.

EE: It gave me a great dislike of popular music. Popular music is awful now and was awful then, but in those days you could hear the words, which made it worse. I'll take 'Chattanooga Choo-choo' to my island but I won't play it, I'll just look at the label and think how peaceful it is if I don't put it on.

(Music)

SL: That was 'Chattanooga Choo-choo' sung by Dame Kiri te Kanawa with the band of the Grenadier Guards.

EE: That's the good-looking Maori woman, isn't it? Chap called Levin has a crush on her. Did you know that?

SL: Everybody knows that. What about your next record?

EE: At my public school they had a music competition every year. We used to have to listen to some precocious scholar sawing at catgut with horsehair and making a noise as if the cat was still alive. One year the voice solo was won by a boy who sang: 'Where'er you walk, / Cool gels shall fan the glade'. There won't be any cool gels on my island, but I might as well have the record.

(Music)

SL: That was 'Where'er you walk' sung by José Carreras.

EE: Where did you find him? He really said 'gels', didn't he?

And so we should go on, through 'Lloyd George Knew My Father' sung by the Vienna Boys Choir, to Lady Thatcher reciting the Gettysbury Address (or whatever it is). This I should put on once a year as my birthday treat to remind me how nice it is to be able to listen to parrots and macaws instead of That Voice. And then:

SL: A luxury item?

EE: A Centurion tank.

SL: Why do you want a Centurion tank?

EE: It's the only tank I know how to work.

SL: But why do you want a tank at all?

EE: In case someone tries to rescue me. The Centurion comes with armour-piercing shells for sinking ships, high explosives for blowing up life-rafts, and a machine gun for finishing off survivors. I don't want my island to be swarming with do-gooders trying to make me go back to a world where they pickle sheep and call it art, and pay legal aid to millionaires.

Then comes the bit when Miss Lawley thanks me for being such a delightful guest.

22 July 1994

Reincarnate the Dead (Languages)

IF EVER I want to induce a feeling of deep melancholy I go to the National Portrait Gallery. You do not need to go far back in time to see what is wrong with us now. Gladstone, Disraeli, the Brontës, George Eliot, Brunel, W G Grace – these are the sort of people who look down from the walls of the Victorian section. Then you go into the modern bit and Paul McCartney stares at you from the back, Iris Murdoch is reproduced five times over on the left, and Robert Maxwell, mysteriously labelled 'Lord Mountbatten', smirks down on the right. Further off to the left you find Lords Home and Attlee and you feel you are in better company until you come upon Lord Armstrong.

They even used to have a better class of leftie. There is a magnificent portrait of John Burns who left school at the age of ten and rose to be President of the Board of Trade in 1914. He is painted in a donkey jacket and the garment becomes him better than ever it did Michael Foot, and he looks as if he became his office better than Michael Heseltine ever will.

Of course they generally had the advantage of being properly educated. If you said in the Victorian room 'Step down from your frame if you know what this means: *radix omnium malorum est cupiditas*,' there would be a rustle and they would all be on the floor, unless they thought such schoolboy learning was beneath them. Any of the moderns who ventured down would probably say it means, 'Money is the root of all evil,' which it does not as *cupiditas* is not the Latin for money.

On which topic, if I were to say, 'Have you five pounds about you?' those who carried so much Victorian money would produce a sheet of beautifully engraved and printed white India paper, while today's generation would be shoving five, 10 and 20 pound notes at me indiscriminately as it is so hard to tell the difference. If I then asked, 'How much is an eighth of a pound?' the Victorians would instantly answer 'Half a crown' while the rest were fumbling for their calculators. If I said, 'How much is a third of a pound?' the Victorians would say 'Six and eight pence – the price of a lawyer's letter,' whereas now you cannot divide a pound by three and a lawyer would hardly write three words for a pound, let alone three letters.

I find it difficult to say whether going over to decimal coinage or giving up the study of Latin and Greek has been the bigger factor in our decline as a nation, but I am sure they go together. The old pound of 240 pence was a work of genius, being divisible by almost everything. We abandoned it for the futile reason that we have ten fingers on which to count. If I had been in charge I would have said that toes, eyes and ears are to come into the calculation, and we should still be dealing in 24s and still be prosperous.

As for Latin and Greek, in my boyhood the Treasury was full of people with double firsts in Classics and we were rich, whereas now it is full of economists and we are broke. The day they dropped Latin as an entrance requirement for Oxford was the day they let in the hooligan element, which has led in turn to their getting into the Cabinet, as a result of which I rather think we are done for.

October 1994

My Next Brilliant Career

I AM THINKING of going in for Public Relations, Corporate Identity and the buying and selling of members of parliament, all of which are obviously extremely easy and very well paid. I am not actually too keen on the lobbying business as there would be contact with venal MPs, but I suppose one could wear gloves. Most particularly I fancy Corporate Identity because I read that Mrs Ian Hislop earned more than Mr Hislop when she worked for some corporate identity specialists called Wolff Olins. She was the accounts director, which I take to mean that she directed other people to send out the accounts, and I think I could manage that.

I read about her in an article in which she figured with a woman whose children are called Caspian and Saskia. Names are obviously the key to this business and given the time again I would have called our first two children Hellespont and Boreas, but it is a bit late now. Perhaps I could borrow a couple for the launch of my new firm, which at first I thought of calling Snilo Flow, as it has the right foreign sound, like Wolff Olins, of which it is a variant. On further thought I decided that Lilies of the Field would be better, as in this business we toil not neither do we spin, we just make money.

I am hoping for a piece of the action at British Gas, where they employ a vast army of consultants to help their top PR man, who is called Peter Sanguinetti. This name is from the root 'sanguine' and is the Italian for Cheeryble. He is described as 'presiding over a staff of 30 corporate staff' – probably corporate dwarfs, I shouldn't wonder, called Brightside, Evergrin, Optimus, Hilarious and the like. Peter Sanguinetti himself is said to be 'bespectacled and permanently cheerful'. Quite right. Exactly what I should have advised had I been consulted.

Among the people who cluster about British Gas assisting Sanguinetti and the 30 dwarfs are the usual old Sir Tim Bell, a Germanic refugee from Camelot called Luther Pendragon, plus 'a shrewd Scot' called Angus Maitland who says 'I don't get involved in the implementation side, only giving advice.' Now that is shrewd, and just how I see things at Lilies. The canny Mr. Maitland 'specialises in personal advice to business leaders', which is something we will also be equipped to handle. I envisage the accounts director sending out

accounts like this:

To considering and advising on the Chairman's dandruff problem	
	£3,000.00
To supplying two (2) bottles Boots Head and Shoulders shampoo	4.52
Contribution to packing and delivery	1,350.00
	4,354.52
VAT @ 17½%	762.04
	£5,116.56

Delivery charges may seem a bit steep to anyone not in the business, but this is because we will never use the post but send everything, including the bills, by leather-clad messengers on motorbikes employed by a wholly-owned subsidiary of Lilies, called Jerkins. (I use the word 'employed' in its widest sense. They will actually be paid for by the government on some youth training scheme. We will just include them in the account.)

The one thing I absolutely guarantee is that our services will be discreet. There will be nothing whatever to show for them, except of course the bill.

February 1995

New Tricks for Old Dogs

I UNDERSTAND THAT many men when they retire get a craving for an office to go to. When I say I understand, I really mean I don't understand as I never felt like that about it. On the contrary, I have found that there are three moments in life when life itself improves: when you leave school; when your youngest child leaves home; and when you leave off work. Once you have achieved all three you are free to do what you want to do instead of what someone else wants you to do, and that is the secret of happiness.

Not everyone feels like that. I met a man who had been in pet-food all his life, and the prospect of retiring to days without Pedigree Chum and never a conference on Kitty Kat Munchies was giving him the shakes. His wife was in the same state at the thought of having him at home. It is for such people that pre-retirement courses are run, and while I never went on one I have found out a few things and can lay down some helpful rules for anyone about to enter that happy state.

Rule One: Do not follow your wife around the house when she is hoovering. This is not only irritating, it is positively dangerous. A friend of mine broke his Achilles tendon by tripping over the hoover flex.

Rule Two: Do not try to talk to your wife between 7.05 and 7.20pm as she is listening to *The Archers.*

Rule Three: You need more rooms downstairs and fewer rooms upstairs. This does not mean that you have to re-build the house, but that you must commandeer a room somewhere in which you can keep out of your wife's way, particularly when she is hoovering or listening to *The Archers*.

Rule Four: Buy all the things you want in your last year of work as you will not be able to afford them when you retire. This is more of an excuse for a spending spree than a statement of fact. If my wife expressed concern at the way I was getting through money, I was able to say: 'Don't worry. People go on courses to learn how to do this.'

Rule Five: Don't do everything together. This is to protect you from getting involved in menial and degrading manual labour. I have seen retired mandarins whom I greatly admired pushing trolleys round supermarkets behind their wives. The ultimate humiliation was that the wife took all the decisions as to what went into the trolley and the husband just shoved it along, being thus

reduced from mandarin status to miserable coolie.

Rule Six: Take a calcium pill every day. I got this from a friend who went on a pre-retirement course costing £1,500, paid for by somebody else. 'What have you learned?' I asked when he came back.

'I have learned that everyone over sixty should take a calcium pill every day.'

'Anything else?'

'No.'

Bearing in mind the cost of the course, in passing on this nugget to *Oldie* readers I reckon that for once at least this column is giving value for money.

March 1995

I do abhor thee, Yoof

MISS VICTORIA COREN wrote the other day about 'that club of people who believe Everything is Getting Steadily Worse'. Where is this club? I want to enrol. Anyone who thinks things are otherwise need only reflect that in the 19th century the losses of the banks from compute fraud were nil, and now they run into billions. Also, regardless of what they do at Barings, I bet they couldn't have done it at all without computers – in fact I bet you couldn't have any derivatives to bankrupt yourself with if you didn't have computers. Now they tell us there is a thing called the Internet, and by Surfing on the Internet you can get as much pornography as you want. So the next advance is to have pornography on tap in every school, and soon in every household, and we are to call it progress.

Of course these inventions are not all bad. My son has had his computer stolen with all his jokes on it and so has Lenny Henry. Furthermore they are breaking into the BBC at Bristol and stealing their computers as well. If there is a move afoot to steal the jokes of all the comedians and give the nation a rest from noise and vulgarity, I am all for it. I wish most particularly they would steal whatever is necessary to sabotage the children's television programmes. Oldies without grandchildren may not realise how terrible these are. Propagating yob culture among the yoof, which is all they do, would be known to the Athenians as 'corrupting the young' and they put Socrates to death for it. Whatever ogres or ogresses are in charge of children's TV deserve a dose of hemlock, and stealing their computers is far too mild.

Torturous Etiquette

According to the Israeli ambassador, for the purposes of interrogating Palestinians his government has authorised 'the use of moderate physical pressure in accordance with the principles laid down by the Landau Commission'. According to a university student called Abdul Nasser all Qaysi, if it happens to you it is like this: 'I was taken to a corridor... he tied me to a pipe with my hands facing outward. He covered my head with a sack. I could not stand... it was impossible to reach the ground and my shoulders seemed to be coming out of their sockets. I was like that for maybe an hour and a half. It was hard to breathe and I felt a terrible pain in my kidney.' Between bouts of such treatment he was chained to a tiny chair and beaten regularly. When his lawyer pointed out the evidence of torture to a judge the reply was, 'He is under interrogation, not on holiday.' After 51 days he was released without charge.

I wrote to the Israeli ambassador to say this was no way to behave. According to Debrett's *Etiquette and Modern Manners* (which my sister gave to me, although I don't know why as I do not eat peas off my knife), I had to end: 'I have the honour to be, with the highest consideration, Your Excellency's obedient servant'. This is a hard thing to do when you're boiling with indignation, but I went by the book, and I hope it has been entered on my credit side in heaven. It is of course possible that the Israeli ambassador, Mr Moshe Raviv, is a decent fellow and is kind to his old mother and all that sort of thing. Let us hope so.

April 1995

Censure the Censors

ONE OF THE shabby tricks that the BBC plays as part of its relentless campaign to corrupt the manners and morals of the nation is to suppress the category, rating, certificate, classification, or whatever you call it of the films they show on television. I am a 12 or U man myself, regard 15 as unsuitable for anyone at all (particularly young ladies of fifteen), and have never seen an 18 or X film and don't mean to start now. PG is simply a species of demented hypocrisy, based on the fantastic notion that parents will go to see films expressly to decide whether they are suitable for their children, as thus:

Kylie: Can I see *Dumb and Dumber*, Mummy?

Mother: Daddy will go after work dear, and let you know in the morning.

The BBC hides all these warnings away and some weeks ago I fell into the trap of staying up to watch *White Mischief*. In the first ten minutes all the women talked like tarts and one of them flaunted her unattractive naked person on the screen, so I put it off. It is as a result of this sort of thing that when I looked through the list of Bafta awards I found that I had not seen any of the things they were giving awards to except *Middlemarch* and the *Grand National*.

I am therefore proposing to institute my own awards, which I thought of calling the Efta (E for being Enfield), but Efta is or was a Free Trade Area; or else Eoka (Enfield's OK Awards) but they were Cypriot revolutionaries, so I will just call them the Edwards, like the Oscars.

Front-running film at the moment is *Little Women*, a lovely film of which the only disadvantage is that it made me cry a lot, which is unmanly, so I had to keep wiping my eyes on my cuff and hoping no one would notice.

Black Beauty proved to be a disappointment as horses are limited in what they can do in the acting line, but the Best Actress award is likely to go to a black beauty called Sergeant Cambridge in *Pie in the Sky*, who has a most expressive face and can speak volumes without opening her mouth. I don't see anyone overtaking Jill Dando for the Prettiest Newsreader Award and unless one of those women who reduce the weather reports to mumbo-jumbo can bring off a coup I see no chance of making a comedy award at all.

I am thinking of inviting onto the judging panel a journalist called Petronella Wyatt, for whom I have conceived an enormous admiration. She explained recently that *Four Weddings and a Funeral*, commonly known as Fwaaf, is no good, commonly stated as Nbg. I knew Fwaaf was Nbg because I read that it starts with beastly expletives, but she found out the hard way by going to see it, and discovered it was splattered throughout with schoolboy vulgarity passed off as jokes. (I am sorry to say that my wife sneaked off to see it while I was better employed and came back saying it was funny, which inspired me with a fear that she might be about to enrol in the Chattering Classes. Not that I know what the Chattering Classes are exactly, but I think they are the sort of people who like Fwaaf.)

Later Miss Wyatt wrote that 'film comedy reached its peak in the late 50s', about which I am sure she is right, as everything peaked in the 50s and has been going off ever since. Then bless me if she wasn't saying that unemployment would be abolished if women stopped going out to work! How true, and wouldn't the world be a better place if the likes of Mrs Currie stayed homed and baked cookies, instead of writing pornographic novels and slandering chickens?

If this piece ever comes to Miss Wyatt's notice (and I suspect that half the *Oldie* readers are journalists wanting to keep an eye on what Richard Ingrams is up to), I hope she will not mind my saying that to read writing of such perceptive elegance from one apparently so young is almost enough to inspire one with hope.

June 1995

Art and Orpingtons

I LIKE TO live as much as possible in the past, finding it altogether preferable to the present, while at my time of life to look to the future is to take a very short-term view of things. It was a surprise therefore to find myself so far ahead of the times when I read in the paper that Jane Shilling is cross with Roddy Doyle and Nick Hornby for saying Anne Tyler is the greatest living novelist, instead of John Updike, Philip Roth or Joyce Carol Oates. I am in exactly the situation that most people will be in a hundred years time, as I have never read a word and could not name a work of any of them.

It may be thought a little hard to condemn them to oblivion without having read them. It is of course possible that there might be an H G Wells or a Somerville-and-Ross among them, but it seems decidedly unlikely that the whole lot are up to that, and altogether more probably that in 2095 their works will be as much read as those of Ouida and their names as well known as that of Mrs Henry Wood. Hazlitt says, and I agree, that 'the dust and smoke and noise of modern literature have nothing in common with the pure silent air of immortality', which makes it an act of startling temerity to label 'great' any writer whose works have not stood the test of time.

Or any other work of supposed art, of course. I remember hearing some sensible Labour MP saying in a debate on the arts that, when it came to the ballet, he did not mind people paying money to see some man jumping about in a pair of ladies' tights but please could he not be told that it was part of his heritage. Likewise I don't mind the Saatchis spending their millions on cartoons from American comics but please could they not call it art until three generations have passed. There might be a danger of the collection being accepted in lieu of death duties by a gullible tax inspector.

Taking which view of things I rarely read modern novels, but I knew I was going to meet a lady called Alice McVeigh who plays the cello for a living and has written a book called *While the Music Lasts*, so I read it. It is all about life in an orchestra, a trifle salacious but very good. Miss or Mrs McVeigh, whichever she is (I find such things are not usually revealed in the heady circles in which I have taken to moving since I joined *The Oldie* workforce) told me she lived in Orpington. This is a place I have never visited and had no ideas about, so I closed my eyes and thought of Orpington, and it came out like this:

'Orpington is inhabited almost entirely by chickens – the famous Buff Orpingtons – which roam the woods and pastures. Such women as there are go out each morning in pinafores and feed the hens and collect the eggs. The rest of their time they spend playing the cello to the chickens to encourage ovulation. The men of Orpington pass the day at the alehouse sucking straws, supping ale, and discussing the price of eggs. An attempt was made to establish a village school but it had to be abandoned as the children proved to be ineducable. Their minds were unreceptive to any idea that was not connected with eggs, and the only work of literature in which they could be got to take an interest was the poem "A Private of the Buffs", which they conceived to be an allegory of a rooster taken to China as the mascot of the East Kent Regiment, and always wept copiously at his unhappy end.' It sounds a nice peaceful place.

July 1995

Lewd Literature, Loopy Lecturers and Limpet Lawyers Lambasted

JOAN COLLINS HAS made the discovery that the 50s 'was a wonderful decade'. She is right, of course, and one of the wonderful things about it was that the book shops were free of the sort of novels that are written by Joan Collins. Not that I read them, but as part of the meticulous research that goes into this column I took one off the shelf in the public library and it fell open at a well-thumbed passage of a startling coarseness which in the 50s would have guaranteed her against getting a publisher. I thought it a bit rich that one who has contributed so much to, and profited so handsomely from, the general growth of pornography should bewail the moral decline of the nation.

Things are going to the dogs at Oxford as elsewhere. I subscribed to the Campaign for Oxford because they said I should and because they promised to spend my money on the teaching of Greek. Then I got a letter saying they were going to put some of it towards a new running track and the rest towards a lectureship in Business Studies. I wrote at once to say that I had no strong views on running tracks but if they were going to fritter my money away on something as useless as a lectureship in Business Studies, I wanted it back, so they sent an apologetic letter promising to spend it on Greek.

I am not at all sure that they are to be trusted. They sent me a thing called *Campaign News* and there was no mention of Greek but it said they had set up a Chair of Language and Communication which they had called the Rupert Murdoch Chair. This presumably is an effort to give Mr M a cloak of respectability, like burying Robert Maxwell on the Mount of Olives, and I hope he is not paying for it with money stolen from the News International pension fund. The first professor is a woman who qualified for the job by spending twenty-seven years 'trekking the globe on the international conference circuit', and is to waste her time researching into 'the influence of newspapers on language' when we all know that the influence of newspapers on language is to vulgarise it.

The sad thing about this woman is that she started out quite respectably as a Cambridge classicist. If she really wanted to do some good in the field of Language and Communication she would put in for a transfer to the Greek teaching part of the university, if it really exists, and lecture on grammar and syntax, if she can remember what they are. If she misses the international conference circuit she can always do a few laps of the new running track to which I may or may not have contributed.

People rarely take my advice and when they do they generally regret it. This time it is different and all oldies should do what I say, though they themselves will not benefit, but their heirs and assigns hereafter. My advice, in a nutshell, is this: if you have made a lawyer your executor, change your will.

I discovered this from a friend whose aunt appointed her solicitor in this capacity, which solicitor is now cheating, shuffling, lying, over-charging, procrastinating and generally behaving in a lawyer-like manner by battening on the estate less like a leech than a vampire. My friend has found out the hard way that the only people who can remove executors from wills are testators, and if they dead at the time it is too late.

Of course you may have appointed a solicitor in whom you have absolute trust on the excellent grounds that you and he were at school together or you play golf with her father. Bear in mind nevertheless that solicitors do many things such as predecease their clients or go to jail, in which case some other member of the firm will arise and take over, who may well be a stinker. If you make your wife and your daughter or your son and your brother your executors, they can hire a lawyer when they need one and fire him if he is a stinker, but if you make one an executor they are stuck with him, come what may.

September 1995

The World According to Mrs Enfield

MY CHIEF WISH in life has always been to be like everyone else, and certainly never to stand out in a crowd; perhaps it was because I was so overwhelmingly ordinary that my mother spent most of my childhood searching the sales for what she called marvellous bargains, which resulted in my school uniform lacking any semblance of uniformity, my shoes far too upmarket for that wonderful squeak which no amount of dubbin would remove, and for which I longed.

From the pinnacle of old age I can see the huge disappointment which my mother must have experienced at producing such a wretched child. Things are supposed always to get worse before they can get better, and at twenty five I was still not married; then came the turning point, I met a pretty reasonable sort of a fellow, and about a year later we were married.

Now, I thought, was my chance to begin a conventional life; we settled down in the country and produced four children, which was a pretty conventional thing to do in the days before you were only supposed to have so many fractions of children. I had been brought up on the old penny catechism, the only piece of which indelibly imprinted on my memory is that the sins against hope are despair and presumption. With four children there was not much chance of presumption gaining ground, but who could have foreseen an ordinary law-abiding person like me falling into such a morass of iniquity in the form of Despair. Then suddenly it seemed, after hoping, even presuming, that things must in the end get better, we were through four teenagerhoods and out into the sunshine again.

Now came the chance of Hope. Still hopelessly unambitious, what I hoped for was that the children would lead conventional lives, marry conventional people in wonderful conventional weddings, and live happy ever after. The first wedding took place in the heart of Africa, so there was nothing particularly ordinary about that. Hope came along again seven years later (there must be some biblical significance here) when the second daughter announced her engagement.

We planned everything fairly carefully, and once the invitations had gone out we thought all we need now do was to wait a little while before we knew everyone who would be coming. It does seem strange that one can go through six decades and still not realise that children, and children's friends, will always manage to surprise you. So when, four weeks later, we had still not received replies from very many of those invited, I asked my daughter if she could possible chivvy them up.

Not long afterwards the telephone rang and an unknown voice asked if I was I. I replied that I certainly was. 'This is Charles. Of Charles and Sarah. About the RSVP.' 'Ah,' I ventured, 'I do hope you received the invitation.' 'Yeah – but I've mislaid it just for the moment.' Pause, while I thought he might volunteer the information we wanted. He didn't. 'I do hope you will be able to come?' 'Oh yeah, certainly we want to come. So can you book us two tickets?'

We had had just about everything printed that we could think of, but no tickets; Should we ask the vicar if the pews were numbered? Should we write to *Bride* magazine and warn them of this new requirement for weddings? We didn't have any more trouble wondering about the guests. In fact one was obviously so keen to attend that he replied no less than three times, in almost identical wording, the third time on the eve of the wedding itself.

When the great day arrived we felt there was really nothing about weddings that we did not know, and my husband (the nice one mentioned above) felt I should set up in the marriage business and make us rich. This was high praise, and I must commend my foresight in removing the labels from the underside of the bride's shoes – it would certainly not have been conventional when she kneeled down in the church to see the price of her shoes advertised to the whole congregation, particularly as they had been reduced not once, but twice, and Hobbs would obviously have liked us all to know.

But it was the bride's father who had made the most important contribution to the whole affair, by insisting that there were to be no coarse speeches, and so it was that the wedding proceeded in its unconventional way, coarseness absolutely missing, and the bridegroom's speech reducing the entire gathering to emotional tears.

That was two down and two to go and I think a total news blackout would be the best course of action for the two remaining. I certainly don't want to be blamed for any actions on their parts. Hope has still not triumphed over despair, though I did receive a small crumb of comfort the other day when I told my son that his aunt, recently widowed, was to be married to a man, a widower too, whom she had known before they were both married elsewhere.

'Well Mum, that is good news, and perhaps when I am seventy I will marry Penelope and make you happy at last.' That really would be the happy-ever-after ending, but I don't really believe in fairy tales, grim or otherwise, and I'm afraid that at the age of a hundred and one I would have little hope of enjoying it.

Thinking I might indulge in a little evangelisation, I bought from our local cathedral shop two bookmarks on which are printed the ten commandments; but it was only when I got them home that I looked at them closely and found that the Americans have even taken them over, and we were being admonished to honor our fathers and mothers and not bear false witness against our neighbors. This seemed to me to be verging on sacrilege so I wrote to the manufacturers, an English company, pointing out that this was not how these words were spelled in the King James version, from which translation they were taken.

I received a polite reply, in which they excused themselves by telling me that they were unfortunately printed in the States where it was cheaper, so they had to market them as they were. For my trouble they kindly sent me three or four further bookmarks, including one with the following prayer on it: 'God grant me the serenity to accept the things I cannot change, courage to change the things I can, and the wisdom to know the difference. – Reinhold Niebuhr.'

September 1995

Aping Art

I RECALL THAT several years ago the Hanging Committee of the Royal Academy accepted a painting by a chimpanzee - a talented chimpanzee no doubt, but a chimpanzee all the same. When they took it they thought it had been painted by a human being and the whole affair was considered to have been a bit of a blunder. Times have moved on, and I expect that now they would accept entries from the monkey house at London Zoo as readily as from graduates of Goldsmiths college, or at least with as much reason. Having, I flatter myself, a bit of an eye for a bandwagon, I thought I might launch upon the world a whole chimpanzee school, with the intention of making an awful lot of money from the sale of the products of the simian salon to the Saatchi brothers and people like that.

Much modern art strikes me dumb, so I needed to collect some suitable terms in which to describe Chimp Art, and it was helpful to read about the paintings in the RA by Lady Sarah Armstrong-Jones. (Not that I suggest she paints like a chimpanzee - she may be better, she may be worse, I don't know). She spoke of the 'main meal of the day for David and I', which tells you she hasn't quite mastered Her Aunt's English, but nothing about her painting). These pictures, it said, 'had a certain mystical magic combined with unbridled awareness', or else it was unbridled magic combined with mystical awareness, I am not sure which. Elsewhere there was a sort of daub by someone else described as 'abstract, reticent and elegant' and I saw at once that what I needed was an art critic's Vade Mecum or Ready Reckoner, with suitable words in columns, to be combined in threes at random. It has been done in other fields but not, as far as I know, for art, so I culled the words from a few reviews and set them out like this:

diverse	unbridled	awareness	abstract
elegant	magic	focussed	conceptual
reticence	raw	cerebral	emptiness
sheer	impulsive	angst	inbuilt
visual	challenge	brash	amusing
zing	bold	beguiling	panache
mystic	haunting	freshness	

Any *Oldie* reader is welcome to use it. When faced with a dead fish or a filing cabinet, by all means say it shows brash conceptual challenge or mystic beguiling emptiness, or anything else you like, as long as you take one word from each column.

Thus prepared, I set about producing some Chimp Art, and my first attempt was, I am pleased to say, an enormous success. My thought was to get a chimpanzee to arrange three sticks of rock and an apple in a composition to be entitled 'Three Sticks of Rock and an Apple' which would symbolise reality as the evasion of meaning, as you might say, (Well, as somebody did say, or something very like it, in the *Telegraph*.) I gave the materials to one Magnus who, to my great delight, scoffed the lot, an example of Chimp Art in action, which combined inbuilt cerebral magic with raw impulsive zing. As the end result was nothing at all we had at a stride progressed beyond Minimalism to Zeroism itself. I wonder whether the Hanging Committee would accept 'Magnus - Nothing at All' if I delivered it to them in an empty paper bag.

October 1995

The Virtues of an Illiberal Education

LORD CHESTERFIELD SAID that 'Westminster School is undoubtedly the seat of illiberal manners and brutal behaviour' but I am afraid things may have gone downhill since then. By the judicious investment of a five pound note in 1944, my parents made me a life member of the Elizabethan Club. This means that I get the Westminster School magazine, which is called the *Elizabethan*, for the rest of my life. However wisely Westminster invested the money, they must have lost on the deal, as by now the postage alone must have devoured the principal many times over.

By means of the *Elizabethan* I have followed the progress of my old school and it has become clear that the whole place is collapsing in a welter of amateur dramatics. The headmaster leads off with the mention of six plays and a drama festival, which latter had eight plays, and there are references to three others elsewhere in the magazine. As far as I can make out these all took place in two terms, so plays occurred at the rate of eight-and-a-half per term.

I give this as a warning to anyone who might have a child or grandchild down for Westminster. Playacting by schoolchildren conveys no pleasure to the onlookers nor any benefit to the performers, who are certainly diverted from their studies and possibly given an exaggerated idea of their theatrical talents, so a taste for the stage is something that ought to be knocked out of a boy, not encouraged. I remember the late Oleg Kerensky going to ask the late J T Christie, then headmaster, for permission to organise a house play, and getting the only sensible answer, which was 'No'. There was one school play in my time, a production of *Everyman* in which I took a small part, and I have no doubt it was rank bad, but at least in my case it made me immune to amateur theatricals for life.

You cannot tell from the *Elizabethan* what subjects they teach nowadays, but in my time in the upper forms it was a choice between Maths, Science, Modern Languages, Classics or History. It will be seen that History is the only soft-centred subject as they had wisely excluded English, so if you were interested in English you did Classics, thereby improving your knowledge of your own language without wasting time on juvenile attempts at literary criticism. (As a result of this rigorous and exacting discipline my vocabulary of literary criticism consists entirely of trenchant phrases such as 'jolly good', 'hopeless', 'frightfully funny', or 'disgusting'.)

I fear they may allow English now as they have a master who is Head of English, but to give him his due he seems a sensible fellow. He writes that, when he began teaching, the phrase Liberal Education 'meant any activity that removed children from the classroom: kicking a ball, showing off on stage, patronising the poor and disabled. The essential point was to close the books (which were necessarily boring) and get out "there" and do something worthwhile."

I think more highly of him that I do of the physics teacher, who rambles at length about a liberal education without getting to a conclusion, but lets one cat out of the bag when he says that 'the stoic retention of Latin prose composition as part of the A level course, a venerable exercise only persisted in by a handful of schools, is one of the last remnants of the strict education that boys originally underwent.' He must mean that at Westminster they have otherwise switched from a strict to a lax education, abandoning the Greek prose and Greek and Latin verse composition on which we passed our time so profitably, to make room for more fashionable pursuits such as showing off on stage and patronising the poor and disabled.

November 1995

Reconstructing Troubadours and Deconstructing Noddy

SOME WEEKS AGO we had a kind invitation to a concert. I saw that one of the pieces to be played was by Bernard Rands (who he?) and was a *Canzone per* Orchestra (what that?). I found from the *Oxford Dictionary of Music* that Bernard Rands was born in 1935 and was therefore probably still alive (bad sign! - good composers are dead). Furthermore, his music is frequently aleatory (what this?). More work with the dictionary revealed that the word aleatory derived from the Latin for a die, (being one half of a pair of dice), and means that the notes occur at random as if settled by the throw of a die. A *canzone*, it said, is a troubadour song.

To take the notes of a troubadour song, jumble them up at random and have them played by an orchestra seemed to be a melancholy undertaking, and I was not looking forward to it. A friend suggested that I borrow a Sony Walkman and listen to Haydn or Handel while this was going on, but I thought that to wear a Sony Walkman at a Promenade Concert might be thought eccentric, and probably rather impolite to our host. When it came to the moment, therefore, I composed my features into what I hoped would pass for an expression of rapt attention and braced myself for the worst.

The sounds, when they came, were like snatches of music interspersed with notes set down on the throw of a die. The audience applauded like anything when it was over and a man in a suit appeared in the middle of the orchestra, shaking hands with everyone within reach and then clapping his hands in all directions, rather like Mr Khruschev applauding himself at the United Nations. It was none other than Bernard Rands, undoubtedly alive, and expressing the enormous enjoyment which he derived from listening to his own composition. Which composition I think might be called 'reverse melody'. I got the idea from some hideous portraits which apparently were not hideous portraits at all, but examples of 'reverse chic'. Likewise reverse melody is a much more agreeable way of describing an aleatory *Canzone per* Orchestra than just calling it a nasty noise.

Among the things I have seen in the paper recently was this on the subject of Enid Blyton: ' "When it's getting really stressful I reach for the Famous Five." says one obviously clever English finalist at Cambridge. "To be able to read something you can completely deconstruct gives you such a feeling of achievement." '

I knew they talked some nonsense on the banks of the Cam, but I did not know it was as bad as this. Whatever is the clever English finalist clever at? Persuading people that he or she is obviously clever I suppose. Job interviews for such people must go like this:

'What gave you your greatest feeling of achievement at Cambridge?'

'I think it was the time I spent deconstructing Noddy.'

'Oh how obviously clever you are. I will hire you at once. Go out and buy some red braces and start work on the trading floor tomorrow.'

December 1995

Book Awards the Waugh Way

I SEE THAT Auberon Waugh, with his customary but still astonishing perceptiveness, has put his finger on a way to make the awarding of the Booker Prize into an event of interest and importance. He says that while he himself has not read the man's book, Salman Rushdie should have had the prize for being 'chased from pillar to post by religious maniacs'. This is the sort of remark that blinds by its own brilliance and it falls to lesser men, such as me, to take it as a text and expand upon it.

First of all it sweeps away any pretence that any of the contending books has any literary merit, and converts the Booker into a sort of consolation prize for literary figures who have had a hard time, or perhaps fallen on hard times. We should then have the Chairman saying things like: 'We are giving the prize to Angelica Knibbs, not because her novel of lust and depravity in the White Highlands is any good – which it isn't – but because she has wet rot in her roof timbers. £20,000 will just about pay the bill.' This is altogether better than using it to boost the flagging sales of some work which no right-minded person would otherwise read.

Secondly it makes it unnecessary for the judges to read the books, which to a large extent recognises what happens already. Reading between the lines (I can think of no other phrase), each judge is faced with a pile of the sort of stuff that constitutes modern novels, of which it is supposed that he or she will read every word. They don't, of course. They skip through this and they flip through that until they come upon one that is so unredeemedly awful that they study it with care in order to build up a cast-iron case against its getting the prize.

When it comes to the judging they are each saying 'I will vote against Gorbal McGovern if you will vote against Bingo M'Dingo' and that sort of thing, and when they look for a compromise candidate as like as not they pitch on a book that not one of them has read. They don't realise this, of course, as they each think the others have read it and don't like to confess that they themselves have not. This is the only possible explanation of this year's choice, which by all accounts is written with a graphic coarseness which makes even hardened reviewers blench, and renders it such that the ordinary reader would only handle it with rubber gloves and tongs. It was more than enough for me to read an interview with the author, the indelicacy of whose conversation appears to be on a par with the indecency of her writing. (I tried to get a bet on that she would win the *Literary Review*'s Bad Sex Award but couldn't find a bookie who would offer reasonable odds.)

The third and final step would be to dispense with books altogether and give it to some public figure who needs cheering up. The Princess of Wales could have it as a sign of the admiration with which she is regarded by all sensible people in spite of the efforts of press and publishers to poison our minds against her. Then they could give it to Prince Charles, who has a way of looking a little downcast, and after that they could use it to console some innocent businessman who had been convicted of arms dealing on the perjured evidence of a Minister of the Crown. There really is an enormous amount to be said for Mr. Waugh's idea.

January 1996

The Piffle of Literary Criticism

I HAVE ALWAYS thought that literary criticism is a lot of piffle, and if I had my way I would stamp out the study of English Literature at university altogether. Anyone interested in the subject should of course study Latin and Greek to get an understanding of their own language and a background to their own literature. I might let a few dons carry out research into aspects of Eng. Lit., but they would have to be kept in All Souls where there are no undergraduates and would not be allowed to teach or lecture, in case they corrupted the youth.

To deviate slightly from the point for which I am aiming, I once picked up from the floor of County Hall, where I was working, a piece of paper advertising a degree course in Greek literature in translation. In my day undergraduates read Homer and Sophocles in Greek and now they do it in English and it is called progress, though what the gain is supposed to be I have yet to learn. It isn't the students' fault. Dr Peter Jones of Newcastle University ran a course in simple Latin in the *Sunday Telegraph*, and told me he got over

1,000 letters from grateful readers who had been deprived in their youth. The trendy idiots who have removed the classics from the mainstream of education are like the lawyers in St Luke: 'Ye have taken away the key of knowledge: ye entered not in yourselves, and them that were entering in ye hindered.' Very likely you can study French and German literature in translation, and be taught by Professors of French who know no French, and Professors of German who are innocent of German – or if you can't now, you soon will be able to.

But to return to the piffle of literary criticism. Dr Johnson's lines 'Let observation with extensive view / Survey mankind from China to Peru,' were said by someone to mean no more than 'Let observation with extensive observation observe mankind extensively'. I didn't know who that someone was, and then I found it was Coleridge. If Coleridge thought like that, he very likely behaved like this:

Scene: Coleridge's study. Coleridge, armed with a blue pencil, is busy improving the *Book of Common Prayer*.

Coleridge (*aloud*): 'Acknowledge and confess' – no, no, just 'confess' will do. 'We should not dissemble nor cloak' – tut tut, plain 'cloak' is quite enough. What's this? 'Assemble and meet together'? Oh dear no, 'meet' is all we need.

Enter Wordsworth.

Wordsworth: I say, Coleridge, I've just written a poem. Want to hear it?

C (*throwing down pencil*): Oh, very well.

W (*reciting*): 'Behold her single in the field
Yon solitary Highland lass...'

C: That won't do, you know. 'Solitary' means the same as 'single'.

W: Never mind that.
'Reaping and singing by herself...'

C: 'By herself'! Of course she's by herself – you've said so twice already.

W: Do be quiet!
'Stop here or gently pass
Alone she cuts and binds the grain.'

C (*screaming*): 'Alone'! Look here, Wordsworth, there's no need to tell us four times that the only person around is this blessed girl of yours. Anyway a Highland glen is not exactly Piccadilly Circus.

Exit Wordsworth in a sulk.

C (*returning to Prayer Book*): 'Requisite and necessary' – oh dear no! 'Necessary' is all that is requisite...

But there is an aspect of that Wordsworth poem which interests me, when it goes:

'A voice so thrilling ne'er was heard
In springtime from the cuckoo bird…'

Is it really complimentary to a young lady to compare her singing to a cuckoo? If a critic wrote 'Callas sang like a cuckoo' I feel she might not have thanked him.

August 1996

On Publicity Girls and Other Birds

BEING AS I am but a simple man I thought that PR was something you did, or perhaps had done to you – a method of gulling the public into thinking better of something or someone than they would if left to judge on the evidence. Not so. It is something you can actually become. I learned this from one of those articles which journalists write to interest other journalists and which interest no one else. It was all about what journalists think of PR firms, which you may think is as dull a subject as you can hope to find, and you would be right. It says that 'Veteran PR Liz Brewer laments the fact that every other girl you meet now has a card that say PR on it.' Why she talk like that I don't know but that what it say in the *Times*. Anyway now I have read it I can see that if I moved in the right circles I should have conversations like this:

'Hallo Liz Brewer, what you do for a living?'

'I am a veteran Public Relation.'

Or 'Hallo, young lady with PR on your card, whose Public Relation are you?'

'Oh no, good sir, you are quite mistaken, for I am a Press Release.' Sparkling stuff, and it says in this article that Julia Carling is 'indicative of the dizzy heights attainable by an ex-PR'. Who she? What dizzy heights? I hope to meet her one day so I can say: 'Hallo Julia Carling, what are you?'

'I am an ex-Public Relation.'

'Wow, that is really dizzy.'

All of which leads me to the subject of pigeons. A man called McDonald at

a PR firm called Clarendon decided that the way to publicise an Edinburgh insurance company was to send 77 pigeons in cardboard boxes to 77 financial journalists. They were supposed to let them go, and win a case of whisky. This is no way to treat a pigeon. Without being a Public Relation myself I could have told them that it wouldn't work – there is a special relationship between the Englishman and the pigeon. Not long ago some chap took to scooping up pigeons in Trafalgar Square and putting them into pies. Every newspaper in the country was full of it, the *Times* alone having six articles about pigeons in one day. That there should be such a fuss cannot be explained in ordinary terms. The pigeon population of Trafalgar Square was not sensibly diminished – if you ask me there are still far too many and in the mass they are rather horrible – shoving and gorging themselves like winged maggots. I cannot believe that if even half the Trafalgar Square pigeons were put into pies the tourist trade would be seriously affected, or that those foreigners who come to London for the pleasure of being crawled upon by pigeons would transfer to St Mark's Square in Venice. The explanation must be psychological.

Clearly we would all really like to keep pigeons but can't because of the practical difficulties. We see ourselves in cloth caps carrying our favourite pigeon to the railway station in a hamper, to be taken by the London and North Eastern Railway to a remote corner of the country and released by a friendly porter. Before the LNER can return the hamper the pigeon is ringing the bell in the loft to announce its safe return. But alas, that is all in the past – there is no LNER, there are no friendly porters, and even pigeons are probably not what they were. Even so, when we encounter a pigeon a wave of nostalgia overwhelms us and we would not harm a feather of its head. We have to keep more practical pets but we do it by default; psychologically speaking, a dog is just a substitute pigeon, and a cat but a pigeon surrogate.

As for shuttling them about London in boxes: 'We are absolutely outraged'

September 1996

Managing the Birt-ish Broadcasting Corporation

I SEE THAT Lord Edward Spencer-Churchill, just down from Cambridge, has been taken on by an American firm to be a management consultant. To be consulted by whom, one wonders, about the management of what? Who needs the advice of an almost beardless boy on how to run their affairs?

'Mr Birt' is probably the answer. As is well known, the BBC is an organisation in the grip of management madness, spending millions of our licence money on management consultants. For those who have not come across the breed, it consists partly of girls with clipboards and partly of men who, like Lord Edward, have never managed anything, or else if they have, have failed. Obviously Mr Birt needs help, but I do not think these are the people to give it to him.

If you ask the nice girl at the right-hand end of the reception desk of Broadcasting House for a piece of scrap paper because you want to copy down the inscription in the hall, she says: 'Would I do that to you?' Then she gets up and starts hunting in a drawer. 'I suppose,' you say, 'that you are going to give me a special superior piece of BBC crested paper?' 'Better than that,' she says, and gives you a copy of the Latin inscription, complete with translation. Of course I cannot say she will always do this, or that it will always be the same girl, or that she will always sit in the same place, but it is what happened to me.

Now I have been reproved by a friend in Salcombe for spraying too much Latin about this column, so I will just give the inscription in English: 'This temple of the Arts and Muses is dedicated to Almighty God by the first governors in AD 1931, John Reith being Director-General; and they pray that good seed sown may bring forth good harvest, that all things foul or hostile to peace may be banished hence, and that the people, inclining their ear to whatsoever things are lovely and honest, whatsoever things are of good report, may tread the path of virtue and wisdom'.

Is it possible to think of any other organisation which in the space of a lifetime – my lifetime – has departed so far from its own ideals? Just before the nine o'clock news a girl puts on a silly voice and says, in effect, 'After the news it's going to be this' and you are shown a clip of something either foul or hostile to peace or, as in the case of a trailer featuring Clive Anderson, unfunny as well.

But never mind, the good news is that the other lot are as bad or worse. I have never heard that ITV has a motto, but if they have it is probably 'Aim Low'. There was a recent gathering of television people in Edinburgh to which the ITV delegates went for the purpose of insulting our intelligence by telling us that we ought to like rubbish and that if we don't we are élitist. 'Journalists do write that programmes are tacky and that is élitist,' goes one quote. 'We live in an age when we have a paedophile ring in Belgium. Surely you would expect some part of our drama to reflect this?' goes another. It is a great consolation that the tacky spectacle of public executions was stopped. If we had such things today the government would have put the job of public hangman out to private tender, Rupert Murdoch would have bought the rights to televise the proceedings and the Home Secretary would be telling us how good it was to have all this money coming in every time someone was strung up.

As the only idea of commercial television is evidently to make money by appealing to the lowest side of human nature, Mr Birt is on to a winner. All he needs to do is kick out all management consultants, everyone not subscribing to the BBC motto and allow ITV a monopoly on vulgar trash, a market in which he has hitherto endeavoured to compete. Having grasped that what we really like is *Yes Minister* or *Middlemarch*, he would win the ratings contest in a canter by recapturing the vast but currently switched-off audience of mature and intelligent people like Mrs Edward Enfield, Terence Rattigan's aunt, and readers of *The Oldie* magazine.

October 1996

McMoney Talks

I READ THE other day the melancholy statement that when it comes to planning applications McDonald's always win, because they have more money than anyone else. Their tricks include hiring expensive lawyers to use prolonging tactics till the opposition runs out of funds. Thus, some councils no longer bother to oppose them, but surrender and save their cash.

All of which makes it all the more delightful to read that they have met their match in a penniless pair called Helen Steel and Dave Morris, who have kept McDonald's at bay in the longest running civil case in British history. For those who have missed it in the press, it is a libel suit. In the manner of R Maxwell (deceased) McDonald's pounced upon Helen, Dave and others, ordering them to recant, repent, and withdraw leaflets they were handing out, upon pain of a libel action and bankruptcy. To which the dauntless pair replied that as they had no money McDonald's could sue and be damned to them.

So, on 28th June 1994, on behalf of McDonald's, Mr Richard Rampton QC strode into court (or trotted perhaps – I don't know if he is big or little) complete with a train of admiring junior barristers, intent on knocking the stuffing out of Helen and Dave. Much of the stuffing so far seems to have been the other way about. The case has cost McDonald's the best part of £2 million and a wealth of bad publicity, but H and D with no case, no legal aid and starting with no knowledge of the law, give every bit as good as they get.

Although they have no money they have expenses, for instance in fetching witnesses from America, so I have enrolled among their admirers and send them small sums of money from time to time. For this I am more than repaid by a news sheet with details of their various triumphs – such as issuing Lord Vestey with a subpoena and making him confess that, although he had written a letter saying the beef he was supplying 'was not coming from reclaimed land from destroyed rain forests', in respect of 90 per cent of it he hadn't a clue where it came from.

There has been so much excitement that I cannot repeat it all, but two points strike me as particularly choice. H and D alleged that McDonald's advertising was misleading, and in support produced this statement, dated 1987: 'The Attorneys General of Texas, California and New York have concluded our joint review of the McDonald's recent advertising campaign which claims that McDonald's food is nutritious. Our mutual conclusion is that this advertising campaign is deceptive. We therefore request that McDonalds immediately cease and desist further use of this advertising campaign. The reason for this is simple: McDonald's food is, as a whole, not nutritious. The intent and result of the current campaign is to deceive customers into believing the opposite. Fast food customers often choose to go to McDonalds because it is inexpensive and convenient. They should not be fooled into eating there because you have told them it is also nutritious.'

Did you ever see such a slap-up knock-down no-nonsense piece of prose coming from, of all people, three senior law officers? Can you possibly imagine the Solicitor General the Attorney General and the Master of the Rolls putting their heads together and producing such a straightforward statement as that? 'No', you will say, and I agree.

McDonald's was thrown into such a panic that they hired private detectives to infiltrate H and D and their friends. The most astonishing thing, though, is not that McDonald's were reduced to this sort of thing but that Special Branch helped them! Sid Nicholson, McDonald's UK vice president, confessed that when McDonald's were picketed in October 1989, a Special Branch officer stood by him passing him information on individuals in the crowd. So that is what Special Branch does! I thought they caught criminals and terrorists, but not so – they lurk about looking for people like Auberon Waugh making rude remarks about hamburger gases.

No doubt, Mr Richard Rampton QC regards H and D as a pair of nice little earners, but I imagine they inspire McDonald's with a mixture of terror and loathing. For which reason I earnestly hope they will set up as anti-McDonald's consultants, as every planning officer in the country will wish to retain them, and their fortunes will be made. Meanwhile, full details of their glorious undertaking can be got by writing to the McLibel Support Campaign, 5 Caledonian Road, London N1 9DX – always assuming that the Special Branch men pass on the letters after they have steamed them open.

November 1996

Horsham's Favourite Son Remembered – In a Nutshell

THE OLDIE REACHES the furthest corners of the civilised world, such as London, Ontario. From there a Canadian journalist who says his name is Inkblot has written to me to say that he thinks Damien Hirst should be pickled in formaldehyde and exhibited at agricultural shows. It seems a good idea and might be called Reverse Art, the exhibiting of pickled artists at cattle shows being the reverse of pickled cows at art shows.

There was a bit of a fuss not long ago when they refused an export licence for a picture by a living artist. I forget which artist, but it seemed to me to be a fault on the wrong side, if you can have such a thing. I would be in favour of exporting a lot of living artists, never mind their art. I suppose the works of Damien Hirst would be caught by the beef ban, but there could be no objection to exporting the artist, even in formaldehyde.

All of which serves as an introduction to the fact that they have put up a memorial to Shelley in Horsham and it looks like a nut. The milk-chocolate-coloured husk is peeling back to reveal an aluminium kernel, and it is of course symbolic. It is also a fountain, but they had to turn it off as it did not work; or to be precise, it worked too well and sprayed the pavement with water which froze and caused the people of Horsham to fall over. The fountain may symbolise the poet spouting, but possibly not, because on the edge are some lines which begin:

The everlasting universe of things Flows through the mind ...

So if you understand that, you may understand why the nut is a fountain, (though possibly not why the fountain is a nut). As well as the big nut there are four little nuts, which may symbolise Shelley's four children; but then again, they may not. It is sited outside McDonald's and, being empty of water, serves as a convenient receptacle for polystyrene boxes.

It is all due to Sainsbury's. For the best part of two centuries the people of Horsham went about their business indifferent to the fact that Shelley was born a few miles away, until Sainsbury's were allowed to desecrate the town with a superstore, and in return gave £100,000 for a 'public work of art'. In consequence Shelley was declared to be Horsham's Favourite Son and they put up a chocolate nut fountain in his honour.

It was inaugurated at a ceremony with the fountain spouting water and Paul

Foot spouting verses written by Shelley and called *The Mask of Anarchy*, which was inspired by the Peterloo Massacre and written in the style of Cyril Fletcher. The poet starts by declaring that he has had a dream, which, from what follows, could well have been brought on by raw pork and opium taken in the company of Keats. Fraud appears personified, inexplicably weeping tears which turn to millstones:

And the little children who
Round his feet played to and fro,
Thinking every tear a gem
Had their brains knocked out by them.

Why a child should mistake a falling millstone for a gem is not explained, but otherwise the Cyril Fletcher style has been very well hit off.

Anarchy arrives, also personified, and
He was pale even to the lips
Like death in the Apocalypse

Which would be well enough if 10 verses later we did not find that:

Anarchy, the Skeleton
Bowed and grinned to everyone

So here we have a fully fleshed skeleton complete with lips and pallor.

The poet is not more happy with his horses than his skeleton. Anarchy is riding a horse, and:

With a pace stately and fast

Over English land he passed.

Now I defy the most accomplished horseman in the Spanish Riding School to ride at a pace that is both stately and fast. It means, if it means anything at all, that Anarchy hurried along slowly. Another horse, the Horse of Death:

Fled and with his hoofs did grind
To dust the murderers thronged behind.

Whatever the product of murderers ground by horses may be, it certainly is not dust. There is plenty more like this, and all in all, I think Paul Foot and the committee are to be congratulated on choosing a poem so entirely appropriate to the peculiarities of the monument.

January 1997

Defects of Character Are as Nothing Compared to the Infirmity of Baldness

I SUPPOSE THAT for those condemned to attend the Tory party conference the thing is given a certain spice by the thought that some editor is probably harbouring a bombshell which he plans to explode to liven things up at a suitable moment. It might be fun to be on the spot when it happened, and one would keep one's ears pricked for the first whisper of a revelation of adultery or perjury or soliciting or drunkenness or bribery or some other example of the worldly and carnal lusts to which the flesh of the MPs generally, and ministers particularly, is prone. There may also be a frisson of excitement from the thought that the Animal Liberation Front or someone like that might blow the whole show to smithereens. I hope, for the sake of those attending, that this is some compensation for the sheer awfulness of having to force a semblance of merriment at the pleasantries of Mr Heseltine, or to suffer oneself to be clapped on the back by men who would gladly pick one's pocket did they but have the skill to do it undetected.

Corruptibility is now the commonplace of politics, and, as Sir Peregrine Worsthorne has pointed out, there is no longer any such thing as disgrace. Men do not retire to the shadows like Mr Profumo, they bluster and swagger like ex-

Ministers of Fun or Defence Procurement. ('Procurement and Fun' sound like 'Pimping and Whoring', but I can't help that.) For Mr Blair, however, things are different because he is going bald and that is something which neither the British Public nor his parliamentary colleagues will forgive.

I, who have not been tried in the furnace, cannot say with certainty that I would not, if asked, trifle with the actualité to send innocent men to gaol; or that I would never hold out my hand for £1,000 to ask a question; or that I would never be picked up blotto from a gutter. I could be counted on as a safe pair of hands if it came to voting for a 26 per cent pay rise for myself and nothing for war widows, but if Pamela Bordes offered to be my research assistant I fear I would accept at once. On these matters therefore I cannot take too high a line, but when it comes to baldness, there I speak with authority. When I think of the lovely ladies with whom I might have stood a chance, or the excellent jobs to which I might have aspired if I had been better off on top, it is clear to me that defects of character are as nothing compared to this particular infirmity. It would have been better for Mr Blair to have been caught hanging about a public lavatory than this. Now the cat is out of the bag I fear that Mrs Blair can roll up those plans for redecorating Downing Street, for they will not be wanted.

Which brings me to the recent case of Mr David Willetts, which has been misunderstood. His is a case of serious baldness. He is said to have been chucked for dissembling, but since when has dissembling been a chucking matter? Cast your mind back to the Scott inquiry. To alter the rules on exports to Iraq, to tell Parliament you have done no such thing, and to sign gagging orders to suppress the evidence - what is this but one big conspiracy to dissemble? And when it all came out did any heads roll? Not one, because unlike Mr Willetts's, all the heads concerned were pretty well covered, whereas he, poor chap, has practically no hair.

February 1997